TOO MUCH STUFF

TOO MUCH STUFF

Capitalism in crisis

Kozo Yamamura

P

First published in Great Britain in 2017 by

Policy Press	North America office:
University of Bristol	Policy Press
1-9 Old Park Hill	c/o The University of Chicago Press
Bristol	1427 East 60th Street
BS2 8BB	Chicago, IL 60637, USA
UK	t: +1 773 702 7700
t: +44 (0)117 954 5940	f: +1 773 702 9756
pp-info@bristol.ac.uk	sales@press.uchicago.edu
www.policypress.co.uk	www.press.uchicago.edu

© Policy Press 2017

British Library Cataloguing in Publication Data
A catalogue record for this book is available from the British Library.

Library of Congress Cataloging-in-Publication Data
A catalog record for this book has been requested.

ISBN 978-1-4473-3565-8 hardback
ISBN 978-1-4473-3567-2 ePub
ISBN 978-1-4473-3568-9 Mobi

Cover design by Lyn Davies Design
Front cover: image kindly supplied by www.alamy.com
Printed and bound in the United States of America

Contents

Preface and acknowledgements

The analysis of capitalism in crisis I present in this book has evolved from two earlier versions, one published in Japanese in 2015 and the other in Chinese in 2016. This book presents the same analysis as is in the earlier versions, using the same examples of the US, Japan, Germany and several other Western European countries, but my argument is reinforced by newly available data and the developments that have taken place since 2013, when I began to write the Japanese version.

However, since I submitted the manuscript to Policy Press in March 2016, numerous, notable political and economic developments have occurred, including Brexit – the UK voting to leave the European Union – and the election in the US in November 2016. The data, both macroeconomic and other data pertinent to my analysis, have also continued to change. These political and economic developments, the changing data since March 2016, plus some reflections on them are summarized in a brief Postscript to demonstrate how they support and even bolster the analysis offered in this book.

I express my sincerest gratitude to the following people who made this book possible. I would like to thank nearly two dozen friends in the US, Japan and Europe, most of whom are economists and some of whom do not agree with various aspects of my analysis. Yukio Noguchi and Guenter Heiduk, two friends, using virtually identical words, said my work is "worthy of debate because it brings up a novel and important insight essential in discussing the crisis confronting the capitalism and democracy of the developed economies of today." The two anonymous referees who evaluated the manuscript for the Policy Press provided me with detailed and valuable comments and criticism that helped reduce errors and significantly improved this book. I am grateful to Alison Shaw, Director of Policy Press, who decided my manuscript with its unorthodox argument was worthy of being peer-reviewed. I am also grateful to Judith Oppenheimer who edited this book, substantially improving the exposition as well as correcting errors. And, finally, Susan Hanley, my wife, representing interested lay readers, spent countless hours to make certain that this book can be read by everyone.

ONE

A new perspective on capitalism's "sickness"

Advanced economies are so sick we need a new way to think about them.

—Lawrence H. Summers,
Professor of Economics at Harvard University and
former Treasury Secretary and Director of the
National Economic Council in the
Obama administration
(*Washington Post*, November 3, 2015)

Introduction

My reason for writing this book is that I believe I have found a new way of thinking about the "sick" advanced economies, one that would help our efforts to reinvigorate the stagnating economies and floundering democracies of the world's most developed countries.

Today, as the developed economies continue to stagnate and disparity in the distribution of income and wealth grows ever greater, a growing number of people are extremely concerned about the future both of the capitalist economic system and of the democratic political system. This book has been written with people in mind who are thinking about such crucial questions as the following.

- What are the reasons for the continuing slow rate of economic growth?
- Why is disparity in the distribution of income and wealth widening?
- Has capitalism become incompatible with democracy? Or has capitalism always been inherently incompatible with democracy?
- Can capitalism's "sickness" be "cured", or must capitalism be replaced with another economic system?
- Why hasn't the fiscal policy of reducing taxes and stimulating investment been successful? Have policies to increase the money supply helped our economies to grow? Or have they benefited only the wealthy?
- If the rate of employment has been increasing, why are real wages stagnant, or even declining, for so many workers?
- Why are the developed economies producing more and more luxury goods and services and at the same time investing much less than is necessary to meet societal needs, such as preventing further degradation of the environment and maintaining or improving the economic infrastructure and education?

I want to reach people who are pondering these and other related questions and explain my ideas, because they elect the politicians who will adopt the policies that are needed to effect change. Although academic publications are valuable in advancing scholarship, they are usually highly technical and are read by only a small number of people. This book is intended for a much wider readership.

Capitalist economies: the realities

Stagnation and its consequences

Before I set out my ideas, I want to note two realities in all of today's developed capitalist economies. The first is the "sickness" revealed in the real (inflation adjusted) growth rate since the 1980s. In the US, the rate of growth of GDP (Gross Domestic Product, the total amount of all goods and services produced) averaged only 2.62 percent from 1980 to

2007. Following the global financial crisis of 2007–08, it fell even lower, to just 1.42 percent between 2008 and 2014. In Japan, the same rate was 2.61 percent from 1980 to 2007 and 1.09 percent after 2008. The average growth rate in Europe's five largest economies (Germany, France, the UK, Italy and Spain) was 2.42 percent before the financial crisis, but it turned negative, at minus 0.65 percent, during the period 2008–14.

For all of these economies, the average real GDP growth rate from 1980 to 2014 was dismally low compared to the 6.4 percent achieved from 1950 to 1979, when they were all growing rapidly, led by Japan in its "high speed growth period" and Germany during its "miracle growth years."

The prospect for the near future of the developed economies remains dismal, and the likelihood that they will continue to suffer from the ongoing "sickness" or is very high. The forecasts of the Organisation for Economic Co-operation and Development (OECD), the International Monetary Fund (IMF) and several other respected organizations are virtually unanimous. All of the developed economies are expected to grow by less than 3 percent in 2016 and 2017. The expected rate of growth ranges, at best, from around 2 percent for the US to 1–1.5 percent for the European Union (EU) economies and about 1 percent for Japan.

In all of the developed economies were numerous undesirable political and economic consequences from the low post-1980 growth rates, including: stagnant real wages; frequent recessions that increase unemployment; much less investment than is necessary to meet societal needs now and into the future; and a growing threat to democracy because of the widening disparity in the distribution of income and wealth.

A new world of necessary luxuries

While most people are aware of this first reality, there is a second reality that is ignored in the ongoing debate about the future of capitalism and democracy. The failure to recognize and confront this reality is the reason why all developed economies have adopted ineffective economic and social policies.

This second reality is that since the 1980s a majority of citizens in the advanced economies have enjoyed the highest living standard known in human history. It is one that even the greatest kings of 200 years ago and the wealthiest people of the 19th century would envy. It is the result of industrialization, which began in the late 18th century and enabled the GDP of industrializing economies to grow by at least 3 percent per year – in contrast with the maximum of 2 percent *per decade* prior to industrialization. The real income of all economies that industrialized grew steadily, led by the US, where the real annual average income of citizens in 2015 was almost 12 times higher than in the mid-19th century.

Evidence of today's unprecedentedly high living standard is the fact that, for the majority of citizens, their needs for the daily necessities of life have been sated. By the 1980s, more and more people were acquiring an unprecedented quantity and variety of luxuries. These include a vastly increased choice of gourmet foods, closets full of clothes, countless new, mostly electric or electronic "toys" for adults and other frivolous things bought increasingly on a whim and for vanity or amusement. And more and more people are living in houses that are larger, better built and better equipped than those of their grandparents, if not of their parents. There are an unprecedented number of services, including numerous modes of virtually instant electronic communication. And many people in the developed economies travel by air for international tourism, and an increasing number do so frequently.

What people first thought of as luxuries soon became necessities, something they felt they couldn't do without. Few people today would be without their smartphone, their microwave oven and many other similar gadgets. No one today thinks of television as the luxury it was in 1948, when there were just over 100,000 TV sets in the US. Today it is just another necessary appliance, as is evident in the fact that some 99 percent of US households have at least one TV set, and the average is more than two.

All this is to say that today a majority of people in the developed economies live in a "new world of too much stuff," in which they are acquiring historically unprecedented amounts and kinds of goods and services that our parents would have considered luxuries but that they have come to believe are "necessary." We will call these goods and services "necessary luxuries."

Necessary luxuries

We need to know two facts about necessary luxuries. First, they have been increasing as a proportion of total consumer demand, which accounts for roughly two-thirds of GDP in all the developed economies. However, demand for these necessary luxuries is growing too slowly to prevent the economy from continuing to suffer from the persistent "sickness" of slow growth, for the following reasons.

- It takes time and money to convince consumers that newly offered goods and services are "necessary."
- Real wages have been increasing very slowly, or even falling, for a portion of the population.
- A slowed rate of population growth, or even a steady decline, means fewer consumers.
- The rapid pace of globalization means that developing economies have been increasing the quantity of their exports to developed economies, thus reducing demand for domestically produced products in those economies.

Because demand for the new necessary luxuries was beginning to grow only slowly, by the 1980s most industries began to experience persistent excess productive capacity. With a decreasing need to expand productive capacity, firms reduced their pace of investment. When this happens, the growth rate of an economy decelerates, and a "sickness" sets in.

The failure of pro-investment policy

In order to try to reinvigorate their stagnating economies, governments began to adopt a fiscal policy of reducing taxes, while central banks pursued a monetary policy of increasing the money supply. Both policies were intended to increase the investment necessary to promote economic growth. However, the advanced economies continued to be "sick" because neither policy can be effective in the new world in which demand for necessary luxuries is growing only slowly.

If these pro-investment policies have proven to be ineffective, why do they continue to be adopted? There are three closely interlinked reasons.

First, virtually no one in the developed economies seems to have realized that we are now living in a new world with an unprecedentedly high standard of living in which a majority of citizens are buying necessary luxuries. This is due to the fact that most people very quickly become accustomed to a higher living standard. In other words, they unconsciously broaden their definition of "necessities" to include more and more goods and services that until recently either were luxuries or didn't exist. Thus, people are disposed to think it desirable to increase investment so as to produce more of these broadly defined necessities.

Second, a large number of people who determine or help to determine economic policies have a strong incentive *not* to acknowledge the fact that we are living in a new world. Politicians, regardless of their ideology, support pro-investment policies that they believe will increase the supply of necessary luxuries in order to win the votes of their constituents. The producers and providers of necessary luxuries, and others who stand to benefit indirectly from the increasing consumption of these goods and services, have an obvious economic incentive not to recognize the arrival of the new world. And economists, who as advisors, central bankers or pundits play a significant role in making economic policy, do not (or are unwilling to) recognize that we are now living in a new world. This is because existing economic theories are designed to help an economy to achieve the highest possible growth rate by using its resources most efficiently in producing *all* goods and services, whether they be necessities or luxuries.

Third, the narrative of these pro-investment policies, which is based on supply-side economics, is supported by a majority of voters because it is more persuasive than competing narratives. So let us look at exactly what supply-side economics is, and then why it appeals to voters.

Supply-side economics and "small government"

Supply-side economics is a credo that maintains that when taxes and interest rates are reduced, the cost of investment will decline. This will result in more investment and employment, more goods will be produced and sold, and this will increase the rate of economic growth, to the benefit of all. Most supporters of supply-side economics maintain that their credo is based on the theories of Adam Smith (1723–90), the Scottish philosopher and social scientist who used the metaphor of "the invisible hand" to describe the social benefits resulting from individuals engaging in economic activities for their own ends. This metaphor became the basis for the supporters of supply-side economics to argue for the necessity of a "small government" – one that taxes and regulates economic activities the least, to the benefit of all citizens.

In fact, Smith used the phrase "invisible hand" only three times in his voluminous writings, and to use the metaphor to justify minimizing taxes and regulations is to pervert Smith's nuanced thinking. When one reads carefully his two principal works, *The Theory of Moral Sentiments* (1759) and *An Inquiry into the Nature and Causes of the Wealth of Nations* (1766), one sees that it is irrefutable that Smith believed government has indispensable roles to play in enabling an economy to function. Government must provide for societal needs, such as infrastructure and education, and must enact laws to regulate business in order to protect workers. And Adam Smith argued explicitly that governments should tax the rich to help the poor. While he considered a market economy a powerful force for the good of society, he definitely was not an advocate of "small government."

The supporters of supply-side economics have perverted the metaphor of "the invisible hand" in order to justify their own political ideology and their political and economic self-interest. When one studies their writings, some scholarly and others punditry, it becomes obvious that each author's ideological preference trumps objective analysis and evidence.[1] The following provides a glimpse of the vapidity and fragility of the origin of the credo that helped to launch the Reagan Revolution for "small government."

> In September 1974, an up-and-coming economist named Arthur Laffer sat down ... with President Gerald Ford's chief of staff and his deputy ... Don Rumsfeld and Dick Cheney. Laffer wanted to explain why Ford's plan to impose a 5 percent tax surcharge was a bad idea. He grabbed a cloth napkin to explain and pulled out a pen, and sketched a doodle that became known as the "Laffer Curve." It showed that when taxes are higher than a certain point, raising rates will lower revenues because people work and earn less. This insight helped launch the Reagan Revolution.[2]

The Laffer curve is an ideologically based and empirically unfounded assertion represented by a doodled graph drawn by Laffer. The graph starts at zero percent tax with zero revenue, rises to a maximum rate of revenue at an intermediate rate of taxation and then falls again to zero revenue at a 100 percent tax rate. The shape of the curve that Laffer drew was such that the intermediate rate yielding maximum tax revenues was significantly less than the prevailing tax rate. The intent of the curve was to provide an "analytical" basis to prevent any increase in taxes, because more taxes would mean a larger government.

If the credo of "small government" is based on an ideologically motivated reading of Smith's book, and if the doodled Laffer curve can be considered as support for it, then why is this pro-investment narrative, based on supply-side economics, more persuasive than all other competing narratives? Hasn't the invalidity of the credo become evident since the pro-investment policies have proven to be ineffective, as demonstrated in the continuing stagnation of the developed economies since the 1980s, and especially after 2008, when these policies have been pursued even more vigorously?

The narrative based on supply-side economics has been successful in obtaining the support of voters mainly because many voters are disposed to think that more investment to produce more goods and services is desirable, and that the more you produce, the more robust the economy will be. They are beguiled by the promise that *lower taxes* and an invigorated economic performance will benefit everyone, and at no cost to anyone.

Alternatives to supply-side economics

Three main alternative narratives have failed to win the political support of a majority of the population. One is communism, which is based on Marxism. This has the support of only a very small number of voters in the developed economies, and for many reasons. The most important among them are people's familiarity with the history of the Soviet Union and the sharply contrasting living standards between East and West Germany and between North and South Korea. And, for many in the West and Japan, communism is an anathema for many other reasons too.

A second alternative is socialism, mainly what is called democratic socialism, which has many supporters, especially in Europe. But since the 1980s, even in Europe, supporters of democratic socialism, such as the socialist parties in Germany and France and the Labour Party in England, have been unable to win elections as often as the conservative parties. The main reason for this is that democratic socialist parties do not promise to reduce taxes, but more often advocate various tax increases. For many voters, the logic of democratic socialism is both less beguiling and less readily comprehensible than supply-side economics.

Yet another, third alternative is the "liberal" capitalist alternative offered by the Democratic Party in the US and similar parties in Europe and Japan (such as the Green Party in Germany and the Democratic Party in Japan). But this alternative has also been politically less persuasive than pro-investment policies, essentially for the same reasons that the democratic socialist narrative has not caught on among voters.

Because of the relative popularity of the supply-side narrative among everyone from voters to politicians, bankers and some economists, even the liberal political parties and the central banks in the developed economies have adopted pro-investment policies. This is exemplified in their continuing support for lower taxes and for vigorously increasing the supply of money so as to reduce the cost of capital – that is, interest rates.

However, despite the fact that such policies have now been in place for several decades, the advanced economies remain in persistent stagnation. And because of these policies, as will be explained in this book, the disparity in income and wealth distribution continues to widen and insufficient investment is being made to meet vital societal needs, including providing adequate social "safety nets" to the needy, maintaining the physical infrastructure and preventing further degradation of the environment. Such a situation should not be allowed to continue.

The central goal of this short book is to offer a new way of thinking.

We need a systemic change

First, we must recognize that we are living in a new world. Capitalism has proven to be the most productive economic system in history, but we must make changes in order for it to survive and thrive into the future. We must realize that since the 1980s most people in the developed economies are living in a new phase of capitalism in which a majority of citizens are sated with daily necessities and are acquiring more and more luxuries that they have begun to believe are necessary. Only when we become aware that we are in a new world does it become obvious why the pro-investment fiscal and monetary policies have been ineffective. Only then will we recognize that what we need to do in order to reinvigorate our capitalist economies and sustain democracy is to make a major systemic change in our capitalist system. *We do not need a new economic system to replace capitalism; rather, we need to change capitalism systemically.*

Making a systemic change is possible. It has already been done twice before in capitalist systems, first in the UK in the

19th century, and then again in the US between the 1890s and 1930s. The changes made in the UK enabled it to avert a revolution that could have occurred due to the excessive disparities in the distribution of income and wealth resulting from the industrialization that began in the mid-18th century. In the US, systemic change reinvigorated the economy, which was plagued by serious political corruption and an immense disparity in both income and wealth, and was then devastated by the Great Depression. The changes enabled the US to become an undisputed economic power after the Second World War, and one that was significantly more egalitarian than previously.

In the case of both the UK and the US, systemic change was achieved by overcoming the determined opposition of formidable and entrenched political and economic powers. The transformation included numerous fundamental changes in laws, institutions and practices, as we shall see in Chapter Eleven − changes that few had initially thought possible.

What is needed in the 21st century is a third systemic change. It will be a daunting undertaking, but to fail to make it would be grave folly. We need to learn from history and recognize that in the new world we now live in pro-investment policies are not only ineffective to reinvigorate the economy but also detrimental. They are increasing the disparity in the distribution of income and wealth, which threatens democracy, and they contribute to the neglect of socially necessary investment.

The contours of the needed third systemic change will be outlined in this book. The change will benefit everyone, including the wealthy, most of whom support pro-investment policies − but they too will profit from a reinvigorated economy. Without systemic change, the democratic capitalist economies will soon pass a tipping point both in the disparities in the distribution of income and wealth and in environmental degradation. Passing the first tipping point will almost certainly bring about political change, either through an election or even by a revolution, that will radically redistribute income and wealth. And passing the second tipping point, that of environmental degradation, will cause a catastrophe, the expected horrendous consequences of which are well known.

Many among the wealthy who deny this impending tipping point are gravely mistaken, for when it is crossed, the value of all of their assets will plummet.

About this book

This book will focus on the three largest economies, those of the US, Japan and Germany, in order to demonstrate that economies with different histories face systemic crisis for essentially the same reasons. Four other large European economies – those of France, the UK, Italy and Spain – will also be discussed as examples of more than a score of other developed economies in Europe, Asia and elsewhere that also face a systemic crisis.

Since this book has been written not for economists but for the general reader, it will make minimum use of jargon and all technical terms will be fully explained. Because most of the data and observations presented can be readily found, the citation of sources is limited to those that cannot be easily verified. Notes citing academic articles and books are limited to those that are especially important to support the specific observation or analysis presented and that some readers may wish to read in order to better understand the analyses. The content of some chapters will be somewhat idiosyncratic because I present my own personal experiences. My hope is that this will help to make the book more readable.

Some readers will criticize analyses and arguments presented in this book because of their ideological bias. However, my hope is that, despite any perceived bias, readers will find the book valuable in considering the questions asked at the beginning of this chapter.

TWO

Inspiration in the Kaufhaus des Westens

Luxury has lost much of its mystique ... A strategic view is critical to striking the right balance among a number of imperatives. To position themselves to thrive in the new world of luxury, companies must manage conflicting priorities in every major aspect of the business. Expand into small but high-growth markets while protecting the foundation in the epicenters of luxury; ... Maintain the iconic look of a luxury brand (young and beautiful) while appealing to older consumer segments.

—Conclusion of the Boston Consulting Group's study for luxury goods producers and luxury service providers, *The New World of Luxury*, December 2010

The middle class is continually striving after things that were once only seen in the hands of the wealthy. I'm sure that many of us can name devices, or types of clothing, or a myriad other things that have not only increased in complexity, cost, and size (or getting smaller in the case of technology), but also have increased in how common they have become

13

... What I am describing here, is the basic human condition which causes us to lust after something that captures our attention. We get to the point where we want it so badly, that we begin to convince ourselves that it is a necessity, and that our lives will not be complete without it.

—Khaleef Crumbley,
"When Luxuries Become Necessities",
Blog, 2013

The goal of this chapter is to explain why I began to believe that we in the developed economies are now living in a new world of necessary luxuries and how I became convinced of the usefulness of this idea in thinking about how to enable capitalism and democracy to survive and thrive into the future.

The Kaufhaus des Westens

Thinking back on it, I have no doubt that the idea came to me in 1999 in Berlin, where I was attending an international conference of German, American and Japanese social scientists. The purpose of the conference was to explore why the German and Japanese economies, which had achieved a very high rate of economic growth during the immediate postwar decades, had become by the 1990s, respectively, the "sick man of Europe" and "an economy in a lost decade."

During the conference, a German friend, whose wife insisted that he should buy something special that he could get nowhere else, took me to the KaDeWe, the Kaufhaus des Westens, which is the largest department store in Europe. Although I had been to many large department stores, the size of the KaDeWe and the number of items offered for sale astonished me. When I asked a senior sales person about the floor space of the store and the number of items for sale, the answer was "I know the total floor space is 60,000 square meters, but I've no idea how may items we sell. I do know that the number is at least twice what it was when I started working here almost 20 years ago."

Going from floor to floor of the huge, six-storey building, I became overwhelmed by the immense number and high quality of the items displayed. As my friend and I ate lunch in the large and crowded restaurant on the top floor, we discussed how the Germans, although now living in a "sick" economy, were rich enough to buy the products sold in the store. I still remember my friend's answer: "Our economy isn't doing well but most of us can afford the things this store is selling even if we don't really need most of them."

During the conference we had wide-ranging discussions about the reasons for the slowed economic growth of Germany and Japan, and I couldn't help thinking about what I had seen in the KaDeWe. Living in the US and often travelling in Japan and Europe, I have been in many large stores and am aware of people buying more and more luxury items. And whenever I visit a large shopping mall I can count very few shops that are selling goods that people actually need.

As the conference went on, I realized that there seemed to be a disconnect between the topic of the conference and the existence of an almost countless number of items for people to buy that aren't necessary, by any rational standard. In short, I found myself thinking, "Not only Germany and Japan, but other developed economies too, are growing distinctly more slowly than during the immediate postwar decades. And from all I read and hear, people in other developed economies besides the US, Germany and Japan are also buying more and more luxurious goods and enjoying more luxury services. How is this possible? Is it possible that the slowed growth and greater spending on luxuries are in some way connected?"

Because I was busy teaching and working on several research projects, this question remained at the back of my mind for several years. Then, with the Great Recession of 2007–08 all of the developed economies began to adopt pro-investment fiscal and monetary policies. As the policies continued into 2013, it became increasingly obvious they were not succeeding, and indeed could not succeed. As I scrutinized the data and read the arguments justifying these policies I became increasingly convinced that they could not be effective because their success depended on increasing investment, and increasing investment wasn't working in the new world for two closely interlinked reasons. First, total demand, which would justify additional investment, was growing only slowly because demand for necessary luxuries was growing only slowly. And second, despite what the supporters of these policies were arguing based on supply-side economics, total demand was not increasing because the policies were not having the "trickle-down effect" that their supporters claimed would make everyone better off.

"Necessary luxuries"

As I began to read what others had written about the consumption of luxuries, I found the following.

Thorsten Veblen, an American economist and sociologist, published *The Theory of the Leisure Class* in 1899. In this book Veblen argues that the rich indulge in the "conspicuous consumption of luxuries" in order to demonstrate their wealth. But the consumption by a majority of people in developed economies of what I call necessary luxuries is fundamentally different from Veblen's conspicuous consumption, indulged in by only a small number of the wealthy. This is because necessary luxuries are consumed by a large majority of citizens in developed economies, and they consider these goods and services necessary, and not luxuries.

Abundant observations and data make it impossible to deny that today, in the economies in which per capita GDP exceeds 30,000 US dollars, the majority of people are purchasing necessary luxuries. The following quotations relating to the US are only a small fraction of the very large number of similar quotations that can be found for the US and other developed economies.

A study carried out by the US Department of Commerce estimates that in 2011, American consumers spent $1.2 trillion on "non-essential stuff" that included pleasure boats, jewelry, alcoholic beverages, gambling and candy. These purchases amounted to 11.2 percent of total consumer spending, up from 9.3 percent a decade earlier and only 4 percent in 1959, adjusted for inflation. In February of 2011, spending on "non-essential stuff" had risen by an inflation-adjusted 3.3 percent from the year before, compared to a 2.4 percent increase for essential things such as food, housing and medicine. (*Wall Street Journal,* April 22, 2011)

Take, for example, clothes. The US apparel industry today is a $12 billion business. According to the Bureau of Labor Statistics, the average American family spends $1,700 on clothes annually. But the dollar figures are of little significance since it accounts for just 3.5 percent of a family's expenses on average. What is significant is whether that money is spent on need or waste. The answer is by and large waste. In 1930, the average American woman owned nine outfits. Today, that figure is 30 outfits – one for every day of the month. (*Forbes*, January 15, 2015)

The average American house size has more than doubled since the 1950s; it now stands at 2,349 square feet. Whether it's a McMansion in a wealthy neighborhood, or a bigger, cheaper house in the exurbs, the move toward larger homes has been accelerating for years. (NPR, Hawaii, July 4, 2010)

One out of every ten Americans rents offsite storage. This is the fastest growing segment of the commercial real estate industry over the past four decades. The self-storage industry in the United States generated $27.2 billion in annual revenues [in 2009]. This segment of industry has been the fastest growing of commercial real estate industry over the last 40 years and has been considered by Wall Street analysts to be recession resistant. (*The New York Times Magazine,* September 2, 2010)

The Waste and Resources Action Program, or WRAP, an anti-waste organization in Britain, reported that "about 60 million metric tons of food are wasted a year in the United States, with an estimated value of $162 billion. About 32 million metric tons of it ends up in municipal landfills, at a cost of about $1.5 billion a year to local governments."

(*New York Times*, February 25, 2015)

Supporting what all the above quotations say – that the new world has arrived in the developed economies – is a 2006 survey by the Pew Research Center. It is entitled "Luxury or Necessity? Things We Can't Live Without: The List Has Grown in the Past Decade." This survey asked what goods Americans believe are "necessary" and contrasted the answers with the findings of similar surveys made in 1996 and even earlier, since the late 1970s.

To cite only a part of the study's findings, we learn that in 2006, 68 percent of people believed a microwave to be necessary, in contrast to 32 percent in 1996. The same figures for car air conditioning are 59 and 41 percent; home computer: 51 and 26 percent; dishwasher: 35 and 13 percent; high-speed internet access: 29 and 0 percent. When the 2006 findings are compared to those for 1983, the percentages for a clothes dryer are 80 and 69 percent; for home air conditioning, 60 and 39 percent; and for car air conditioning, 59 and 28 percent.

The survey's conclusion was: "The old adage proclaims that 'necessity is the mother of invention.' These findings serve as a reminder that the opposite is also true: invention is the mother of necessity. Throughout human history, from the wheel to the computer, previously unimaginable inventions have created their own demand, and eventually their own need. But you don't have to take our word for it – just ask the American public."

Indeed, no one can deny that rapid technological progress, especially in electrical and electronic technology during the past several decades, has been important in increasing the number of necessary luxuries. However, this is only part of the story. Today more and more such necessary luxuries are "created" and increased also by advertisement, peer pressure and economic policies that will be discussed in the chapters to follow.

The following quotation shows how, by the 1980s, it had become easier to buy necessary luxuries:

> Before the 1970s, our homes were places of quiet and refuge, where we could not be separated from our money. That changed in 1976 with the advent of L.L. Bean's mail-order catalog that enabled consumers to call toll-free to place their orders, and later with TV's home shopping networks. Nowadays, the Internet allows people to easily spend away their paycheck at home, on the road, or even while they're at work *earning* money. And while advertisements used to appear exclusively in magazines and newspapers, today they are everywhere: on bathroom stall doors, airplane tray tables and even laser-etched on the shells of eggs.[1]

And we all know that buying anything, including necessary luxuries, has become much easier because the spread of personal computer and other electronic devices has been exponentially increasing internet shopping or e-commerce.

The number of items carried by stores of all types has been increasing very rapidly. To cite just one example, the number items carried by the average American supermarket quadrupled from around 10,000 in 1975 to a little over 40,000 in 2013, mainly because stores were selling a growing number of varieties of the same product.[2] Of course, one way to read this statistic is that the difference among variations of the same product has increasingly become more make-believe or fatuous than substantive.

This is made evident in a blog of October 21, 2015 entitled "Why Too Much Choice Is Stressing Out" [sic] by Stuart Jefferies.

> Tesco chief executive Dave Lewis seems bent on making shopping in his stores less baffling than it used to be. Earlier this year, he decided to scrap 30,000 of the 90,000 products from Tesco's shelves. This was, in part, a response to the growing market shares of Aldi

and Lidl, which only offer between 2,000 and 3,000 lines. For instance, Tesco used to offer 28 tomato ketchups while in Aldi there is just one in one size; Tesco offered 224 kinds of air freshener, Aldi only 12 – which, to my mind, is still at least 11 too many.

Persistent lack of demand

Advertising is the principal means by which firms "create" demand for their products and services to "give consumers what they never knew they wanted." According to Statista, the statistics portal, by 2013, total American advertising expenditure had reached nearly $330 billion, or 2.2 percent of US GDP. This sum is about the same size as the Greek GDP for its 11.4 million people, or nearly 2.5 times the amount the US government spent on education in 2013. Readily available data for other rich economies also shows large and growing advertising expenditures. Among the large developed economies, Japan has the lowest ratio of advertising expenditure to GDP, but in 2015, advertising amounted to $60.17 billion, a little over 1 percent of Japan's GDP. This is equivalent to three times the GDP of Afghanistan with its 32 million people, or approximately $5 billion more than Japan's allocation for education in its budget for 2015.[3]

Advertising expenditures have had to increase in order to stimulate demand because, in the new world, the utilization rate of the productive capacity of industries in the rich capitalist economies has been low, and since the 1980s, with very few exceptions, the trend has been downwards. For example, in the G7 (the US, Japan, Germany, France, the UK, Italy and Canada) the average utilization rate has generally been constant at around 80–85 percent. Not surprisingly, when these economies suffered a recession, the utilization rate in most industries fell to as low as 60–70 percent of capacity. Simply put, since the 1980s, the rate of production of industries in the G7 countries has remained well below capacity because of a persistent shortage of demand.

The case of the automobile industry illustrates this best. The 2014 data for all of the world's automobile producers show that they produced a total of 86.59 million cars. But they could have produced at least 26 million more by using all of their productive capacity. This explains why manufacturers are forced to resort to many familiar types of sales promotion strategies to sell their cars and thereby increase the utilization rate of their productive capacity. The fierce competitiveness of the industry because of its chronic excess capacity is the reason both for Volkswagen's elaborate scheme to cheat the emission standards test, which came to light in September 2015, and for Mitsubishi Motors' admission in April 2016 that it has been falsifying the test data since 1991 in order to be able to claim that its cars are more fuel efficient than they really are.

The same situation exists in most service industries. To be sure, we all know occasional instances of excess demand, such as the difficulty of getting an appointment or a reservation for various services. But we also know that these are exceptions that prove the prevailing reality of excess capacity in most service industries. The chronic excess capacity of restaurants, hotels and numerous other service types of businesses is the reason why firms face intense competition and why there is a higher rate of bankruptcies in this sector than in others. Data also show unequivocally that in most service industries wages remain even more stagnant than in other industries, and rates of unemployment and underemployment have also been consistently higher since the 1980s.

It is important to stress here that there are other significant reasons why demand has been growing only slowly besides the failure of pro-investment fiscal and monetary policies, which will be discussed in the following two chapters.

Changing demographic trends

First is the change in demographic trends. In the developed economies, the total fertility rate (or TFR) has been on a downward trend since the 1980s. The TFR is the average number of children each woman has during her lifetime, and it needs to be at least 2.1 in order to maintain a stable population. During most of the immediate postwar decades in the rich economies it was about 3.0, but during the 1970s it began to decline. By 2014 the TFR in the US had declined to 1.86, although the total population has been rising, thanks to immigration. But in Germany, Italy and Spain, the TFR has declined to between 1.4 and 1.5; in the U.K it is 1.9. Only in France was the TFR above 2.0 in 2014, as a result of effective government policy for increasing the birth rate. But at 2.08 it is still slightly below the critical 2.1 needed to maintain the population. Japan's TFR has declined to between 1.2 and 1.4. As a result, Japan now faces the dual crises of a rapidly aging and fast declining population. Thus, in all the rich capitalist democracies, either a very slow growth or a steady decline in population has been and will continue to be a significant reason for a slowed increase in demand.

Unequal distribution of income

Since the 1980s, the number of citizens who are able to buy necessary luxuries has decreased because of the steadily increasing inequality in the distribution of income, as will be fully discussed in Chapter Five and also in separate chapters that examine several of the developed economies. Here, just a few facts are presented to illustrate the importance of the effect of increasing disparity in income distribution on the rate of growth in demand for necessary luxuries.

Like all of the other developed economies, the US has a national program to aid individuals and families with low or no incomes. This is the Supplemental Nutrition Assistance Program (SNAP), which in 2015 provided $125.35 per month to each eligible person. Individuals or households whose income is less than 130 percent of the income of the Federal Poverty Level are eligible for SNAP. Thus, for example, a family of four earning less than $2,552 per month in 2015 was eligible. The number of recipients of this assistance program and its predecessor, the Food Stamp Program, has risen from 23.4 million (about 10 percent of the total population) in 1980 to 46.3 million in 2015, or nearly 15 percent of the total population. Quite simply, this means that increasing numbers of the poor are forced to forgo necessary luxuries in order to obtain the necessities of life.

Negative balance of trade

Still another reason for the slow increase in demand is that during recent years imports have continued to exceed exports in the US, the UK and France. Italy and Spain maintain a small positive trade balance of less than 1.2 percent of GDP – but much less than the trade surpluses they enjoyed during many years before the 1980s. Even Japan, which maintained a large trade surplus until 2011, now has a trade balance that fluctuates between a deficit of 1 percent of GDP and a surplus of less than 0.5 percent of GDP. The reality is that imports have been increasing as a trend in these countries to reduce demand for domestically produced products. The only exception is Germany, which consistently maintains a large trade surplus. However, as will be discussed in Chapter Nine, this is achieved at the cost of suppressing domestic demand by reducing the rate of increase in real wages, thus increasing the number of the poor in Germany.

Conclusion

Although demand for goods has been increasing only slowly, everyone, from governments and central banks to producers and sellers of goods, has continued to promote the production and sale of necessary luxuries and stuff of all kinds. Despite this, doubt has been growing among the public about the wisdom of buying and owning the plethora of possessions that clutter our lives. For example, Japanese magazines have devoted whole issues to storage and "de-cluttering," advising people to consider the value of the floor space a new purchase will fill. Marie Kondo's bestselling book in Japanese on "tidying up" has become a *New York Times* bestseller.[4] Advice from numerous authors focuses both on how to organize our myriad belongings and also on how to get rid of many of them and simplify our lives, thereby improving our quality of life. Kondo advises us to dispose of up to 60 percent of our rarely used possessions, many or most of which are clearly necessary luxuries. In the US, the magazine *Real Simple* was launched by *Time* in 2000 and currently claims 7.6 million readers. But, while the theme of the publication is to live simply, the irony is that it is supported by the advertising industry, so that much of the content and emphasis is on products we are urged to purchase.

As consumers, we are befuddled. We are confronted daily with advertising for necessary luxuries, and peer pressure to buy the latest styles or goods, and shopping has become a favorite pastime. So we drift through malls, visiting store after store selling things we don't need, purchasing stuff from salespeople whose earnings are barely above the poverty level. We buy "new" products and throw out the "old," instead of using ones that are nearly identical to the "new" and still perfectly useful. Nor do people repair broken appliances, which often costs more to do than purchasing new ones. Hints of thrift and "make do and mend" have become passé. The "new" things do not improve the quality of our lives, but we are urged to buy anyway.

Our current economic system depends on our purchasing these necessary luxuries, and so, as citizens, we are in a bind. For firms to survive and succeed, they must constantly sell more necessary luxuries, no matter how unnecessary and wasteful they are. Planned obsolescence, changing fashions, making trivial functional changes and adopting many other "marketing strategies" to promote sales have become widely accepted practices. Even people living on the poverty line are suckered into buying brand-name sports shoes for their children while their diets remain inadequate.

The purchase of necessary luxuries continues while we neglect to make socially necessary investments to maintain and improve the social infrastructure and "safety nets," prevent the further degradation of the environment and do many other socially necessary things, as will be discussed in Chapter Six. To my knowledge, no social scientist or pundit, whether of the Right or the Left, has yet realized the arrival of the new world. No one has yet written a book analyzing what economic policies should be adopted in order to reinvigorate the economy and democracy in the new world of too much stuff. Because politicians are eager to please voters who are always desirous of buying more and more necessary luxuries, as will be discussed in the next two chapters, we have been adopting fiscal policy focused on tax cuts and ultra-easy monetary policy that are both ineffective, as is seen in the continuing economic stagnation and the failure to make socially necessary investments.

THREE

Unreal tax rates

Introduction

Since the 1980s, all of the advanced economies, one after another, have adopted a pro-investment fiscal policy that has reduced taxes, especially income and corporate taxes. The ostensible goal of this policy, which is based on supply-side economics, is to enable investors and companies to have more money to invest and thus to produce more of their products and services in order to increase the growth rate of the economy.

The annual reports of the OECD, an organization of 34 advanced and emerging economies, contain data that document the tax policies of OECD member states. The annual report of 2015 concluded: "The trend across OECD countries, has been towards a reduction in top statutory PIT [personal income tax] rates, inclusive of surtaxes and sub-central income taxes. The OECD-wide average top statutory PIT rate decreased significantly in each of the last three decades, from 1980 to 2014."[1] The OECD data also support this statement printed in *The Economist* of February 25, 2012: "Corporate tax rates across the OECD have fallen by as much as half since 1980."

The US

Among all the developed economies, the US and Japan have pursued this policy of tax reduction the most steadily and aggressively. First, let's look at the US, where the highest income tax rate from the 1950s through the 1970s remained above 70 percent. It was as high as 91 percent between 1954 and 1963, but by 1982 had been reduced to 50 percent. Then, in 1988, it was reduced substantially, to 28 percent. Although the rate was increased to 39.6 percent in 2000, it was reduced again in 2003, to 35 percent, but was raised once again to 39.6 percent in 2014.

However, none of these rates is the effective rate – that is, the rate at which income tax is actually paid. Volumes of studies have shown indisputably that the effective tax rates are significantly lower for many of the wealthiest taxpayers because of numerous provisions in the tax laws that enable them to reduce their tax payments. Most Americans are familiar with what Warren Buffett, the second-richest man in the US, has repeatedly said: "My effective tax rate is significantly lower than that of my secretary." The Congressional Budget Office has supported Buffett's observation. It has estimated that the average effective income tax rate in 2014 for the top 10 percent of taxpayers was 20.7 percent, and only 30.6 percent for the top 1 percent of incomes.

The lowest corporate tax rate in decades

Just as the personal tax rate has been drastically reduced in the US, so has the corporate tax rate. It stood at 50 percent during the postwar decades, but in 1981 it was reduced to 46 percent, and then in 1986 to 34 percent. In 1993 it was increased by one percentage point, to 35 percent. However, more importantly, numerous studies reveal that the average effective rate has been on a downward trend since the mid-1980s. For example, the *Wall Street Journal* reported on February 3, 2012 in an article entitled "With Tax Break, Corporate Rate is Lowest Rate in Decades" that "US companies are booking higher profits than ever. But the number crunchers in Washington are puzzling over a phenomenon that has just come into view: Corporate tax receipts as a share of profits are at their lowest level in at least 40 years." The article stated that the effective rate was 12.1 percent. The number cruncher revealing this was the Congressional Budget Office. *Time* magazine reported on February 8, 2012: "America has the second highest corporate tax rate in the rich world. But most American businesses don't pay it. Indeed, most are paying much less. Indeed, 115 of the companies in the S & P 500 paid less than 20% in tax over the last five years. And 39 firms paid less than 10%." And the April 9, 2016 issue of *The Economist* reported, "The 50 largest listed firms in America paid global tax equivalent to just 24% of their pre-tax profits in 2015."/

The low effective tax rate for corporations is mainly the result of a large number of loopholes, exemptions and special provisions that have enabled firms to avoid corporate taxes. Many readers will be familiar with the recent numerous news reports in the US relating to many large firms, especially multi-nationals, paying corporate taxes at a very low effective rate or even avoiding them altogether. For example, Boeing, General Electric and Verizon were among the 26 profitable Fortune 500 companies that paid no corporate income tax during the period 2008–12. And in 2014, the 15 very profitable companies that collectively made $23 billion and paid no corporate income tax at all included such well-known names as General Electric, Mattel, Owens Corning, Time Warner and Xerox.[2]

Japan

In Japan, although the conservative Liberal Democratic Party has dominated politics since 1955, the highest marginal rate of personal income tax, including both national and local taxes, remained at 88 percent until 1974. But then it was gradually reduced until in 1984 the highest rate was 65 percent. Then, in 1999 it was reduced to 40 percent. Remember that these are nominal rates and not the effective rates. The latter are significantly lower because of numerous "standard deductions" that increase with the amount of income earned and that consist mostly of broadly defined expenses related to earning income. For example, in 2013 the Ministry of Finance reported that highest effective rate was around 26 percent, rather than the nominal rate of 40 percent.

The corporate tax rate in Japan has also declined, from 43.3 percent in the 1950s to 40.87 percent by the mid-1980s, and 35.6 percent in 2015. These rates are inclusive of the taxes levied on firms by local government. Numerous studies in Japan have shown that, as in the US, the effective corporate tax rate is significantly lower because of various means of tax avoidance allowed by tax law. To cite just one example, the transcript of a debate in the Lower House of the Japanese Parliament on May 22, 2012 contains the following incontestable observation by a Communist Party member: "According to a sample survey made by the National Tax Bureau, the effective corporate tax rate on the largest firms with capital exceeding 100 million yen was only 21.2 percent [in 2011], even lower than the effective rate of 25 percent paid by small and medium sized firms with capital of less than 1 million yen."

Germany

A very similar fiscal pro-investment policy has also been vigorously pursued in Western Europe, where tax rates are higher than in the US and Japan. For example, in Germany, as in the US and Japan, the rate at which tax is actually paid by higher-income earners is significantly lower than the nominal rates. In 2014, the nominal marginal tax rate on the highest earners remained high, at 47.5 percent, because of the so-called "solidarity surcharge," levied at a rate of 5.5 percent. (The surcharge, on both income and corporate taxes, is a special levy introduced in 1991 to finance the cost of the unification of Germany.) However, when the effective marginal rate in 2014 is calculated using the tax data, it was only 29.3 percent because of an increase in the number of deductions allowed. Although the Social Democratic Party (SPD) is in the coalition government led by Angela Merkel's conservative Christian Democratic Union (CDU), it has not succeeded in gaining CDU approval to introduce a wealth tax (*Reichensteuer*) on the highest income earners.

Again as in the US and Japan, in Germany the nominal tax rate on corporate profits has been declining. Despite the rising profits earned by many firms, due largely to increasing exports and suppressed real wage levels, the tax rate on corporate income is significantly lower than it was in the 1980s. The total tax on corporations – the sum of the federal tax and the state "trade tax" – was in the range of 40–38 percent between 1985 and 1988, but had declined to 37–36 percent by 2007. And in 2008 it was reduced again, to today's 32–29 percent range.

As in the US and Japan, the effective tax rate on corporate profits in Germany is significantly lower than the nominal rate, due to various exemptions, deductions and other means of tax avoidance. In the Grand Coalition agreement signed on December 20, 2014 by the CDU and the SPD, minimizing tax avoidance by both German and international firms in Germany was specifically stressed as a goal of the government. Various news reports support the observation made by *Der Spiegel*, an influential German magazine: "Because wealthy business people and companies shift millions of euros abroad to evade corporate and income taxes, the estimated effective rate of corporate tax is about 21 percent and is significantly lower than the nominal rates."[3]

While the effective rates of tax on income and profit declined, in Germany the rate of the regressive sales tax (VAT) rose from 16 percent to 19 percent in 2007. As a result, in 2014 VAT contributed 30.2 percent of the total tax revenues, as compared to 40.3 percent contributed by income and corporate taxes.[4]

Since the 1980s, as the narrative for pro-investment fiscal policy has continued to win political support in virtually all of the developed economies, conservative governments have pursued and liberal governments have been forced to adopt a pro-investment policy of reducing taxes. But, as we saw in the data presented in Chapter One, there is *no empirical evidence* to demonstrate that reducing taxes has increased the growth rates of economies. However, this result should surprise no one, even though the supporters of supply-side economics continue to argue that a pro-investment fiscal policy enables an economy to achieve a higher growth rate. Supply-side economics is fundamentally flawed, as the following demonstrates.

The downward trend in interest rates

The interest rate on a 10-year government bond is considered to be the benchmark for the cost of capital in a capitalist economy. In the US, this rate has continued to decline since the 1980s, if with occasional volatility. It dropped from a 13.9 percent peak in 1981 to 3.4 percent in 2007, and that was even before the unorthodox, super-easy monetary policy was adopted in 2008, which reduced the rate thereafter to around 2 percent. As will be discussed fully in the next chapter, because of the ultra-easy monetary policy pursued since the Great Recession of 2007–08, the rate has continued to decline, reaching as low as 1.7 percent in the spring of 2016.

In Japan, the interest rate was around 8 percent in 1980, but fell to below 2 percent before the current massive injection of cash by the Bank of Japan was begun in 2013. The rate in April 2016 was around *minus* 0.05 percent because the Bank adopted a negative interest policy in January 2016, as will be discussed in the next chapter. Rates in Europe fell similarly during the period 1980–2008 before the European Central Bank too adopted a super-easy monetary policy that reduced the rate to around 0.75 per cent in the eurozone economies. In the UK, the rate fell from 14 percent in the early 1980s to around 1.4 percent in April 2016, and in Germany it fell from around 11 percent to around 0.095 percent during the same period. Of course, the rate that firms must pay for loans also declined, following the benchmark rate.

However, despite the drastic fall in interest rates, many supporters of a pro-investment fiscal policy have continued to argue that firms have been unable to borrow money at an interest rate that is low enough to enable them to make investments. This is a totally spurious argument. Since the 1980s, and especially since the mid-1990s, firms in the developed economies have continued to hold huge amounts of "internal reserves," meaning cash and near-cash, that is, short-term financial papers that can be readily sold. In 2015, the 500 largest firms in the US, held around $2 trillion of internal reserves, while the 400 largest Japanese firms held approximately $2.2 trillion. The total amount of internal reserves held by firms in the five largest

European countries (Germany, France, the UK, Italy and Spain) exceeded $2 trillion in 2015, with German firms alone having internal reserves in excess of $1 trillion. These are reliable data obtained from the central banks.

It is also important to stress that reports on the availability of bank loans in the developed economies reveal that, since the 1980s, even small and medium-sized firms with fewer than 300 employees have had difficulty obtaining bank loans *only when* prospects for their business were diminished, such as during and a few years following the Great Recession of 2007–08. This unsurprising conclusion is supported in many reports in English, German and Japanese. Typical of their findings is the statement made by a respected research organization, the US National Federation of Independent Business: "In preponderant instances, firms, large or small, would be denied a loan by a bank only when their sales are declining without a prospect of reversing the trend anytime in near future."[5] In the complex capital markets of the developed economies, one can find exceptions to this, but they are too few to justify the pro-investment fiscal policy based on supply-side economics.

The data revealing a continuous fall in interest rates since the 1980s is evidence that the supply of bank loans or low-cost capital has not been a reason for slowed investment and stagnant economies. Neither was a labor shortage the cause of slowed investment and the low economic growth rate, as will be discussed in the chapters to follow.

Thus we must conclude that in the new world of burgeoning necessary luxuries, *firms have been reluctant to make investments, not because of difficulties in obtaining capital or labor, but because of the shortage of demand for their products and services.* This means that the developed economies have been beset by a vicious cycle of insufficient demand, firms becoming saddled with excess productive capacity and diminished investment.

Liberal politicians and conservative fiscal policy

But one question remains. Why do so many liberal politicians support, or accede to, the conservative pro-investment fiscal policy? This is an important question because so many liberal politicians and political parties have de facto acceded to, or even initiated, a pro-investment policy. In the US, the trend of declining income and corporate tax rates began during the Reagan administration (1980–87) and accelerated during the George W. Bush administration (2000–09), and was not reversed during the Democratic administrations of Clinton (1993–2001) and Obama (2009–17). The same trend also continues in Western Europe. Typifying the European trend is the UK, where tax rates were reduced for the wealthy and firms during the Conservative Thatcher administration (1979–90). But the reduced rates were not reversed during either the Blair administration (1997–2007) or the Brown administration (2007–10), when the Labour Party was in power.

The trend toward declining tax rates continues even in France, where the current Socialist government reneged on its campaign pledge to reverse it; instead, the government is now adopting various conservative economic policies. The following quote from the *Christian Science Monitor* of January 13, 2014 aptly summarizes the Hollande administration's U-turn in economic policy.

> Since the president's New Year address, Hollande spoke of a "responsibility pact" with businesses that would include lower taxes and less bureaucratic headaches if they commit to more hiring ... Leftists dubbed Hollande a sellout, nicknaming him "François Blair," after the centrist prime minister in Britain. He is also said to be like Gerhard Schroeder, the German leader from the left who was responsible for pushing through a business-friendly reform agenda that center-right German Chancellor Angela Merkel today reaps the benefits from.

In Japan, the trend of conservative economic policies has continued since the 1980s because the conservative Liberal Democratic Party has remained in power since 1955 – except for two periods totalling less than seven years (1993–1996; 2009–12), during which two weak conservative coalition administrations and the conservative-leaning Democratic Party were in power.

Broadly restated, the reason why liberal parties in the developed economies have been unable or unwilling to reverse the trend is political necessity. The strength of conservative parties in election outcomes since the 1980s has forced liberal parties to accept essential parts of the pro-investment fiscal policy in order to increase their chances of either retaining or capturing power.

Conclusion

Thus, the advanced economies continue to implement this ineffective fiscal policy, which increases the disparity in the distribution of income and wealth. They do this despite the fact that what is needed to reinvigorate the economy is not more money for firms to invest, but more demand for products and services. They ignore the fact that firms in most industries are saddled with excess productive capacity and have very large internal reserves, making it unnecessary to reduce corporate taxes.

The policymakers of these economies are disregarding – or are forced by political necessity to disregard – the following facts. There is no need to reduce taxes on firms and the rich, because there is no shortage of investment capital in the new world, where the need to increase productive capacity is limited by slowly increasing demand and the existing excess productive capacity in many industries. Demand is increasing slowly because an increasing number of people in the middle classes have become unable to buy necessary luxuries because of stagnating incomes. At the same time, the growing numbers of the poor have become unable even to buy necessities, let alone necessary luxuries. In short, three and a half decades of a supply-side pro-investment fiscal policy have proven to be a failure in all the developed economies.

FOUR

Printing money

Introduction

As developed economies in the new world continued to stagnate, even while their governments adopted a pro-investment fiscal policy based on supply-side economics, at the same time their central banks adopted a pro-investment monetary policy, also based on supply-side economics. This policy consists of the orthodox ultra-low, near-zero interest rates and the unorthodox "forward guidance" and "quantitative easing" (QE) and even a negative interest rate policy (NIRP).

Let's first define the elements of this pro-investment monetary policy. Forward guidance is making a de facto promise not to raise the interest rate until a specified or implied future date. QE is when a central bank buys government and private financial assets (mostly bonds) from banks and other financial institutions with electronic cash. This enables banks and other financial institutions to hold additional funds, on top of their legally required reserve, thus allowing them to make more loans. QE is thus tantamount to a central bank printing money in order to buy debt instruments from financial institutions. NIRP is charging a de facto fee for a part or all of the deposits that financial institutions make into the central bank. The intent of NIRP, like QE, is to motivate financial institutions to make more loans.

The Federal Reserve Bank of the US (the Fed) began QE in November 2008 and undertook it in three waves between 2008 and 2014, buying government bonds and other bonds at an average rate of about $30 billion per month. When QE ended in October 2014, the total had exceeded $2 trillion. And although QE had ended, the Fed continued its policy of ultra-low (near zero percent) interest rates.

The Bank of England and the European Central Bank (ECB) have also continued their ultra-low interest rate policies. The Bank of England began QE in 2008 by buying £200 billion of bonds, consisting mostly of UK government bonds. It continued to purchase increasing amounts of government bonds, the total exceeding £375 billion by the end of 2012. The ECB began QE in March 2015, at the pace of $70 billion per month, by buying the government bonds of the eurozone economies. The ECB's QE is set to continue until March 2017, or longer if necessary. By September 2016 the ECB's projected total purchase of government bonds and other financial papers is expected to be around €1.3 trillion. The Bank of Japan also has an ongoing QE that began in April 2013. It is injecting cash into the economy each month in an amount that, when adjusted for GDP, is more than double the amount that the Fed has injected into the US economy since 2008.

The Bank of Japan also adopted NIRP on January 29, 2016, putting it into effect on February 16. This policy charges a negative interest rate of 0.1 percent on banks' deposits ("reserves") at the Bank of Japan. The ostensible goal of Japan's NIRP is the same as that adopted by the ECB in 2014 and the central banks of Denmark and Sweden in 2012 and 2009, respectively. That is, to increase bank loans to firms by increasing the cost to banks of not making loans by keeping their money deposited at the central bank.

As a result of these policies, by the end of 2014, the total amount of money injected into national economies by the Fed, the Bank of Japan, the Bank of England and the ECB exceeded the equivalent of *$6 trillion*. And the amount continued to grow during 2015 and the first quarter of 2016 because of the ongoing low-interest, ultra-easy monetary policies adhered to by the central banks.

This chapter will argue the following: *There is no objective and credible economic theory that supports the ultra-easy monetary policy described above as an effective means of increasing the growth rate of the developed economies.* This policy has not only proven to be ineffective, it has also had numerous serious and undesirable consequences that will be described later in this chapter. Despite this, the policy has been adopted and maintained because a large majority of economists, including central bankers, support it, and because the governments of the developed economies favor or even actively solicit this policy. The Japanese government did so openly in December 2012 when Shinzo Abe, the newly elected prime minister, replaced the governor of the Bank of Japan, who was unwilling to adopt an aggressive QE policy. His replacement, Haruhiko Kuroda, was eager to adopt an ultra-easy monetary policy.

Ultra-easy monetary policy

The central banks' justifications for their ultra-easy monetary policies are no more than wishful thinking or educated guesses that the policies will reinvigorate the economy by increasing investment. This is hardly surprising, because central bankers are economists, and economists don't have a common, empirically supported macroeconomic theory that explains how fiscal and monetary policies work.

Ben Bernanke justified the Federal Reserve Board's position in 2010, when he was Fed chairman, as follows:

> This approach [the Fed's ultra-easy monetary policy] eased financial conditions in the past and, so far, looks to be effective again. Stock prices rose and long-term interest rates fell when investors began to anticipate this additional action. Easier financial conditions will promote economic growth. For example, lower mortgage rates will make housing more affordable and allow more homeowners to refinance. Lower corporate bond rates will encourage investment. And higher stock prices will boost consumer wealth and help increase confidence, which can also spur

spending. Increased spending will lead to higher incomes and profits that, in a virtuous circle, will further support economic expansion.[1]

Haruhiko Kuroda, the governor of the Bank of Japan, explained why his bank had adopted the policy in a statement made in 2013:

> The Bank of Japan has decided to adopt an unprecedented monetary policy. The goal is to double the monetary base – the amount of money in the economy – within two years by buying government bonds and private financial papers. The bank will buy about 70 percent of the government bonds sold every month. The new policy will raise the expectations of the market and firms that deflation will end within two years and low long-term interest rates will continue to decline, increasing investments and the rate of economic growth.[2]

A third justification for this policy is that of the Bank of England, as described by the *Financial Times*:

> The Bank of England has defended its policy of quantitative easing, despite admitting that the top 5 percent of households has benefited the most.
>
> Since March 2009, the Bank has tried to stave off recession by buying £375bn of government bonds, known as gilts. The aim has been to cut their returns, forcing investors to put their money elsewhere, such as in shares. Although pension funds have suffered as a result, the Bank says most people are better off because of QE. By pushing up a range of asset prices, asset purchases have boosted the value of households' financial wealth held outside pension funds, although holdings are heavily skewed, with the top 5% of households holding 40% of these assets.[3]

Let's examine these three statements.

Bernanke's argument in essence is that the Fed policy will promote investment because of "the wealth effect," that is, higher stock prices will initiate "a virtuous cycle" of increasing their value and that of other assets; increased investments by the holders of these assets will raise the growth rate of the economy, increasing profits and wages to the benefit of everyone; and increased demand will increase investment. But, as we saw in the data presented in Chapter One, a policy dependent on wealth effects cannot be effective in the new world we are in because, as the persistent slow economic growth proves, what is needed is not increased productive capacity but more demand, which can be increased by making investments to meet societal needs.

Kuroda's view is also dependent on wealth effects, which do not promote investment in our new world, as is seen in the continuing anemic growth rate of the Japanese economy since the adoption of his policy in 2013. Chronic deflation in Japan cannot be terminated "within two years" by increasing the money supply. This is because, in the new world, demand for necessary luxuries grows only slowly and Kuroda's QE, which has been raising asset prices, has not increased the real wages of most workers.

Likewise the Bank of England's policy, which also relies on wealth effects, has been ineffective. What it has done is to increase the disparity in the distribution of income and wealth, as the *Financial Times* noted.

The lack of a common macroeconomic theory

The justifications for adopting an ultra-easy money policy reflect the following two facts. First, central bankers do not have a shared, credible macroeconomic theory. And second, like all economists, they are unaware that their economies are now in a new world, one in which pro-investment policies no longer work. Here we will present three observations that attest the validity of the first fact.

Three Nobel laureates

In 2013, three American economists, all leaders in the field of macroeconomics, received Nobel Prizes for their principal work. In his, Eugene Fama argued that the prices of assets (stocks, bonds, properties and so on) may be unpredictable in the short term, but in the long term the free market *always works efficiently* so that there can be no "bubbles" (speculative increases in the value of an asset not justified by economic fundamentals) in asset prices. This theory by Fama and others, known as "the efficient market hypothesis," was first advanced in the late 1960s. It provided conservative political and business leaders with an important theoretical basis for waging a successful political battle for the deregulation of the financial market during the 1980s. Today, few people doubt that this deregulation was a major cause for the Great Recession of 2007–08 and its grave aftermath.[4]

In sharp contrast, Nobel laureate Robert Schiller maintained in his major work that, because of "crowd psychology," asset prices do not move in predictable ways and that asset price "bubbles" do occur. The third laureate, Lars P. Hansen, specializes in highly complex statistical analyses of macroeconomic data. He admitted in his principal work that macroeconomics has made "a little bit of progress" but "there is yet much more to be done."[5]

The analyses by Fama and Schiller are fundamentally contradictory, and Hansen sees macroeconomic theory as being only in its infancy. The fact that they shared the Nobel Prize in 2013 is evidence that there yet is no established macroeconomic theory.

A careful review of academic journals in economics during the 1970s and 1980s reveals that liberal economists were slow to criticize the efficient market hypothesis of Fama and others. When they did, their criticism was muted. There is little doubt that this is an important reason why the deregulation of financial markets proceeded during the 1980s. The reason for this slow and muted criticism is obvious. It is difficult for liberal economists to criticize a hypothesis that is supported by the foundation of their discipline: "The market works."

This foundation also shapes the culture of *all* economists, making even the most liberal of them diffident about criticizing international agreements to liberalize trade, and hesitant to support legally mandated minimum wages and laws to eliminate gendered differences in wages.

The Jackson Hole meeting of 2014

At the annual conference sponsored by the Federal Reserve Bank in Wyoming – often referred to as the Jackson Hole meeting – in August 2014, Fed Chair Janet Yellen maintained the following: the US economy still needed help in the form of ultra-low interest rates because the labor market continued to suffer from a tepid rate of wage increases and millions were still unemployed or underemployed. She said that when inflation had yet to become a problem, the current monetary policy, which she believed would increase employment and real wages, should be sustained.

However, news reports on the conference revealed that reactions to her view were sharply divided among economists who attended the meeting. Conservative economists, such as Martin Feldstein, a Harvard economics professor and the chairman of the Council of Economic Advisors under President Reagan, were "hawks," who expressed serious concern that rapid inflation would soon begin if the current monetary policy were not abandoned. In contrast, liberal economists, such as William Spriggs, chief economist for the AFL-CIO, observed that "inflation does not cost as much as unemployment. If, for a while, you have 3 or 4 percent inflation or maybe even 4.5 percent, that is fine because we are so far away from full employment."[6]

Disagreement in the policy committees

In all central banks dissension often occurs among the members of the policymaking committees. Since the minutes of these meetings are published, we know, for example, that at the Fed committee meetings during the last several years at least one member, and often a few of the 10 voting members, has dissented on the kind or timing of a policy change.[7] And at the meeting of the Bank of Japan in November 2014, when the bank decided to increase the money supply by buying even more government bonds and other financial instruments, and in January 2016, when NIRP was adopted, the vote of the committee was five to four, and two of the dissenting members publicly lambasted the decision.[8]

These three examples leave us in no doubt that economists do not share an empirically tested, credible macroeconomic theory that is necessary for analyzing monetary and fiscal policies. They are thus forced to rely on wishful thinking or educated guesses, which are strongly colored by their own ideological tendencies.

Neoclassical economic theory

More broadly, it is important to be aware of the basic characteristics of neoclassical economic theory, in which virtually all of today's economists have been trained. (The adjective "neoclassical" distinguishes it from the "classical" economic theory from which neoclassical theory evolved, starting around the mid-19th century, and also from Marxist economic theory.)

The limitations and weakness of neoclassical economic theory are well known. The principal goal of the theory is to help an economy achieve the highest possible growth rate by using its resources as efficiently as possible. For this reason, economists typically fail to distinguish the nature of products and services produced (such as the difference between necessities and necessary luxuries). This growth imperative of neoclassical economic theory leads economists to propose or to endorse policies that will increase GDP, even when doing so will increase the disparity in the distribution of income and wealth, and to ignore other serious consequences. Most important among them is detrimental effects on the environment. To produce more goods and services means to continue to degrade the environment. Thus, as will be discussed in chapters to follow, societal investments that do not degrade the environment and that include the goal of preventing further degradation of the environment must be made.

Markets play the central role in neoclassical economic theory, but market outcomes reflect the existing distributions of income and wealth, and market participants do not include future generations. This means that neoclassical economics accepts the existing distributions of income and wealth and is therefore not value/ideology neutral. Further, neoclassical economic theory is incapable of analyzing the needs and interests of future generations, such as protecting the environment for them and not saddling them with a huge national debt.

Of course, there are economists who are aware of these weaknesses in their discipline and offer analyses that account for them. But their analyses are not in the mainstream, and it is mainstream analyses — those that are typically made using abstract mathematical models and on the basis of numerous assumptions (such as markets are competitive, market participants have equal access to information, cultural differences do not matter) — that are valued most highly in the profession.

Thomas Piketty, the French economist whose book *Capital in the 21st Century* will be discussed in Chapter Five, observed:

> To put it bluntly, the discipline of economics has yet to get over its childish passion in mathematics and for purely theoretical and often ideological speculation, at the expense of historical research and collaboration with other social sciences. Economists are all too often preoccupied with petty mathematical problems of interest only to themselves. This obsession with mathematics is an easy way of acquiring the appearance of scientificity without having to answer far more complex questions posed by the world we live in. (p. 32)

And in discussing the limitations of neoclassical economics, the late Yasusuke Murakami, who taught economics at the University of Tokyo and who was well known for his broad command of the literature in social sciences and philosophy, wrote:

> Economics, as a body of scientific theory, made errors and is often removed from reality. It has, nevertheless, become a theory that commands respect. The effective use of deductive reasoning in economics has made it a self-contained theory capable of determining the outcome of our debates. However, as Marxist economics came to overwhelm economic thinking in socialist countries, in capitalist economies, the deductive reasoning of neoclassical economics relating to the efficacy of markets has ended up having characteristics similar to those of a monster.[9]

The ineffectiveness of ultra-easy monetary theory

Returning to the pro-investment, ultra-easy monetary theory, let us stress the following very important facts and reasons why this policy is ineffective and has grave detrimental consequences.

Currency depreciation

Ultra-easy monetary policy, especially QE, has the inevitable effect of devaluing the currency of the country adopting it. Although central bankers will not explicitly admit this obvious fact, when they adopt this policy they are engaging in a blatant beggar-thy-neighbor devaluation policy. This is because currency depreciation helps to increase a country's own exports at the expense of the exports of other countries competing in the international markets. This is the reason why Japan's aggressive QE policy has been vociferously criticized by many countries, especially by Germany and South Korea, which compete with Japanese products in many markets.

We should learn from the bitter experiences of the past, especially from the Great Depression of the 1930s, when many countries engaged in competitive devaluation. All devaluing countries lose. Within a country, devaluation benefits only those firms that are exporting their goods, along with their employees and shareholders, and only so long as the countries that are importing their products do not devalue their own currencies. All others lose, because currency devaluation increases the cost of imports and foreign travel. Currency devaluation also creates distortions in markets, thus making an economy less efficient, just as fixing the price of anything does. To think that selling one's own products and services more cheaply for the benefit of a country's own exporters will make everyone better off in the long run is a fallacy.[10]

The impact on emerging economies

The QE policy is a beggar-thy-neighbor policy in another significant way. A part of the $4 trillion of cash with which the Fed has flushed the market since 2008 was invested abroad, especially in emerging economies, by American financial institutions, firms and individuals. This was because they already had more than enough cash to meet their investment needs at home because of sluggish demand. While the emerging economies were receiving American investment, they benefited from it, but they were made to pay a very high price for it. When the Fed began to "taper down" its QE in September 2014, it triggered a sudden and rapid withdrawal of American investment in the emerging economies. For example, from September 2014, as American investments were reduced or repatriated, Brazil, Indonesia, India and other countries experienced a sudden fall in the value of their currencies.[11] These countries now had difficulty paying for imports that were suddenly more expensive and had to raise their own interest rates, at the cost of slowing investment and raising their unemployment rates.

Since 2014, the Bank of Japan's aggressive QE policy has steadily increased the outflow of Japanese money in the form of loans and investment, mostly into the emerging Asian economies. Sooner or later, when the Bank of Japan begins to "taper down" its QE, the countries that are now benefiting will face similarly harsh consequences.

Asset price bubbles

When a central bank increases the supply of money by adopting ultra-easy monetary policy, this will lead sooner or later to "bubbles" in asset prices because people have so much "cheap" money with which to buy assets. Bubbles always burst, and with all the serious consequences with which we are familiar and of which there are numerous historical examples. The following are a few more recent examples.

In the late 1980s, Japan adopted a historic easy money policy, but in 1990 the central bank was forced to suddenly decrease the money supply (see Chapter Seven for a full discussion). This caused the stock market bubble to burst in 1991 and ushered in a stagnation of the economy that still continues today. Japan's Nikkei index was near 40,000 in 1990, but in the spring of 2016 it still hovered at around 17,000.

A second example comes from Spain. Because of the bursting of the real estate bubble in 2008, by 2011 the major Spanish banks were on the verge of collapse, due to the huge numbers of non-performing loans on their books. They had to be rescued by a European loan that allotted them up to €100 billion. If the banks had collapsed, the Spanish economy, already reeling from the effects of the burst bubble, would have been much harder hit. The bursting of the real estate bubble was mainly the outcome of excess borrowing by Spanish banks on the international capital market, which had money to lend at low interest rates because of the low interest rate policies of the central banks of the developed economies.

In the US, stock prices plummeted in March 2000 (the bursting of the dot.com bubble) after several years of a super-easy monetary policy pursued by then Fed chairman Alan Greenspan (1987–2006), who was a devotee of supply-side economics. The Fed reacted to the collapse by reducing the crucial federal fund rate to 1 percent.

The Fed took two years, from June 2004, to raise the rate back to 5.25 percent, which it did in 17 increments of

0.25 percent each. During the two years prior to this raising of the rate, housing and credit bubbles continued to expand rapidly, fueling the pace of increase in household debt and consumption, sharply reducing household savings and increasing the current account deficit to a record level. The very slow increase in the federal fund rate was a significant cause of the Great Recession starting in 2007, although the Fed denied that the recession occurred because of the lack of regulatory oversight on financial institutions.

We can categorically say that all bubbles occur because of an increased money supply and the "irrational exuberance" of investors that is abetted by a sustained ultra-low interest rate policy.

Negative interest rate policy

Negative interest rate policy has various negative consequences that include asset bubbles. For example, in Denmark, since NIRP was adopted, the long-term interest rate for housing loans has plummeted, creating a real estate boom that benefits speculators. Thus, in November 2015 the government had to limit real estate loans by requiring a down payment of 5 percent of the purchase price of houses. The boom increased the difficulty for most Danes of buying a house, while the NIRP has not had the intended effect of helping to end the ongoing deflationary trend and increasing the economic growth rate above 1 percent.

When we examine the post-NIRP economic data for Japan, we find that the interest rate on 10-year government bonds had fallen to around *minus* 0.05 percent by March and April of 2016, and major banks had cut the rate for real estate loans to 0.9 percent. However, as of the end of April 2016, there was no evidence that NIRP had had any effect on the amount of loans made by banks.

Governor of the Bank of England Mark Carney, who has adopted an ultra-easy monetary policy, observed the global economic conditions and criticized NIRP at the 8th Annual International Financial G20 Conference in Shanghai on

February 26, 2016. Note that he used the carefully oblique phrasing of central bankers.

> The global economy risks becoming trapped in a low growth, low inflation, low interest rate equilibrium. For the past seven years, growth has serially disappointed – sometimes spectacularly, as in the depths of the global financial and euro crises; more often than not grindingly as past debts weigh on activity. Ultimately, for monetary policy ... to bridge to a better equilibrium, it must be reinforced by other policies. That is, the low interest rate environment puts a premium on domestic and international policy coordination.

For those central bankers who believe in supply-side economics and are unaware that we are now in a new world, NIRP is a policy of desperation. Despite all the erudite-sounding justifications offered for NIRP by some central bankers, it is against common sense. Why should anyone believe that a policy will work that is based on lenders paying interest on loans that they make to borrowers?

The risk of falling government bond prices

An ultra-low interest rate policy achieved by QE and even by NIRP reduces the cost of government debt, as noted above. This means the government can be less concerned with the burden of the national debt and the need to reduce it. But if the national debt continues to increase, investors will lose confidence in government bonds, so that at some point their price could plummet. The interest rate on the bonds would then skyrocket, plunging the economy into a fiscal crisis and political upheaval.

Here the case of Japan serves as a warning to other developed economies.

Because of the extraordinary QE policy that the Bank of Japan has been following since 2013, the rate of the benchmark 10-year bond remained at around 0.3 percent through 2015, despite the fact that Japan's debt to GDP ratio was by highest in the world, at 245 percent at the end of 2015. because the Bank of Japan is currently buying more than half of the government bonds issued, some of them long-term bonds, the benchmark rate remains low and, as noted above, had even become negative by the spring of 2016. Because the rate was so low, from 2013 to 2015 the government was able to "finance" as much as 40 percent of its budget by selling bonds. In 2016 the budget will be "balanced" again by selling government bonds in an amount equal to 34.5 percent of the budget.

But, unlike during the 1990s, when foreigners owned only a few percent of all of Japan's outstanding government bonds, by 2015 foreigners and foreign financial institutions owned nearly 10 percent. As the government continues to sell more bonds, it courts a growing risk that foreign bondholders who purchased bonds speculatively will suddenly decide to sell off their bonds. This is because foreigners are much more likely than the Japanese to react to a looming fiscal crisis. The sudden selling-off of even a small percent of bonds by foreign bondholders could trigger a collapse of the bond price and a major fiscal and political crisis in Japan.

Difficulties of ending the policy

Ultra-easy money policy cannot continue indefinitely. However, most individuals who purchase an interest rate-sensitive item, such as a house or car, or who hold stock and other assets, hope it will continue, as do the financial institutions that make loans and trade assets. When a central bank announces its intent to end the policy, the result is a sudden increased volatility or a decline in asset prices, and even declining sales of interest rate-sensitive items. Thus central banks are certain to face pressure from politically strong financial institutions and many politicians to continue the policy. So, central banks could be forced to continue their ultra-easy monetary policies, increasingly risking an asset bubble and encouraging the government to sell more bonds and court inflation. /

i the distribution of income and wealth

rate policy increases the disparity in the
ome and wealth by increasing the price
:tional amounts of which are held by the
icing the income of retirees and many others
it on interest income to supplement their
limited m........ r example, a report from McKinsey Global
Institute in December 2013 estimated that because of the Fed's
ultra-low interest rate policy, US households cumulatively lost
$360 billion between 2007 and 2012, compared to what they
would have earned if interest rates had followed their pre-
recession trends. The report noted that the effect of the Fed
policy was "whopping" and "extremely regressive."

In ending this list of the costs and undesirable consequences
of printing money, we need to add two more important
considerations.

Positive interest rate is indispensable lubricant

Positive interest rates are an indispensable lubricant in the
financial system, and there is a reason why rates have been
positive since the capitalist financial system came into being
almost three centuries ago. Ultra-low or negative interest
rates mean that there is little or no lubricant, thus effectively
depriving the financial system of the ability to function
normally and effectively.

We know this because the data show that when interest rates
are near zero, banks, the central cog in the financial system,
can make only greatly diminished profits That is because banks
make a profit when there is a difference between the rates paid
to depositors and the rates paid by borrowers. When the interest
rate is negative, banks holding government bonds yielding a
negative interest rate incur a loss. When banks are only able
to make much diminished profits or even incur a loss, they
are exposed to the risk of becoming unable to perform their
principal function in capitalism: intermediating between savers
and borrowers.

No less significantly, insurance companies, another crucial cog in the financial system of the developed economies, are also adversely affected when interest rates remain extremely low or negative for an extended period. This is because insurance company revenues are determined principally by the long-term investments they make. Thus, when their revenues continue to fall because of a sustained ultra-low or negative interest rate, they will become increasingly unprofitable. For example, if life insurance companies that support the retirement of millions of people are to remain profitable, they must raise the cost of their insurance to such a high level that fewer current and future clients are willing or able to pay for it. This means insurance companies will become unable to pay policyholders who bought their insurance in the 1980s and 1990s, many of whom have been guaranteed annual returns of at least around 4 percent. The longer the current, misguided monetary policies continue, the more precarious the survival of insurance companies will be.

The fallacy of composition: more price competition, less inflation

To date, the Bank of Japan's super-easy monetary policy of the past three years has failed dismally, especially in raising the rate of inflation to 2 percent. Nor have the ultra-easy monetary policies of the Fed, the ECB and the Bank of England been able to increase the rate of inflation by 2 percent, which is their policy goal. This goal is based on the widely accepted view that deflation slows economic growth because, during deflation, demand slackens as consumers are prone to postpone purchases, anticipating a further decline in prices. And producers, knowing this and that mild inflation raising sales prices will make their business more profitable, are discouraged from making investments.

However, it is important to realize that in the new world of "too much stuff," or "necessary luxuries," in which a persisting shortage of demand (excess productive capacity) has become the norm, printing more money does not lead to inflation as expected by "in-the-box" monetary theory. This is because in the new world, each producer is forced to compete to reduce the price (or to maintain the price but improve the real or perceived quality of the product). But it is logically impossible for all producers in a market to reduce their price relative to that of all other producers in a market. If each producer reduces the price of his product or service *vis-à-vis* the reduction in price he expects his competitors to make, the average price of the product will fall, but the relative price of each producer will remain the same as before. This is "the fallacy of composition" – making the false assumption that something that is true for one (a person or a segment of all) is true for all. In the world of "too much stuff," this fallacy continues to be committed, preventing the ultra-easy monetary policy from raising the consumer price index even by 2 percent.

Despite the fact that all of the above should be evident, many economists, mainly conservative but also many liberal economists, have been arguing whether increasing the inflation target of central banks would help achieve a desired – mostly 2 percent – rate of inflation. For example, Koichi Hamada (an emeritus economics professor of Yale University and the senior economic advisor to Japan's Prime Minister Abe) argued that: "The policy that should be adopted is self-evident from economic common sense: So long as there is no inflation, the best policy is to continue an easy monetary policy."[12] Given the futility and the undesirable consequences of the easy monetary policy enumerated in this chapter, plus the inability of raising the CPI by the recent ultra-easy monetary policy, Hamada's view is gravely mistaken in the new world we live in. What we need is not to print more money but to create demand by making investments to meet societal needs.

Conclusion

The argument supporting ultra-easy money policy relies on the premise that the policy will create wealth effects to increase investment and demand. This is a misguided argument based on supply-side economics. In the new world, the demand that is necessary to reinvigorate the developed economies can be increased by making investments to meet societal needs. Increasing the supply of money in order to create the wealth effect – raising asset prices to make the rich richer, on the premise that they will invest more to increase the growth rate of the economy for the benefit of everyone – is a serious folly on the part of persons who remain unaware of the fact that we are now living in a new world of too much stuff.

FIVE

Inequality and discontent

Wherever there is great property there is great inequality. For one very rich man there must be at least five hundred poor, and the affluence of the few supposes the indigence of the many.

—Adam Smith,
The Wealth of Nations

Introduction

In the four years after the Great Recession ended in 2008, the top 1 percent of Americans, who own nearly half of all stocks, received 95 percent of the total income gains reported. In 2012 alone, the top 1 percent saw their income rise by nearly 20 percent, while the income of the remaining 99 percent of the population rose by only 1 percent.[1]

An increase in disparity in the distribution of both income and wealth also occurred in all the other developed economies, though not to same the extent as in the US. This increase in inequality since 2008 has accelerated a trend that began in the 1980s. As a result, by 2011 all of the developed economies were beginning to experience social unrest and numerous protest movements.

The Occupy Movement

The Occupy Movement is probably the best known of the movements. It was a protest against the wealth possessed by the top 1 percent and was started in September 2011 by about a thousand people who occupied Zuccotti Park, near New York's financial center. The pervasiveness of the discontent was evident in the speed with which the movement spread in all developed economies, even though there were no leaders and communication relied on the internet and mass media reports. By early 2012, there were Occupy Movements in about 600 cities in the US, 900 in Western Europe and a dozen in Japan.

The demand of the protesters was the same everywhere: to eliminate or reduce the huge disparity, which they perceived as unfair and unacceptable. But the occupiers had diverse ideas on how to achieve their goal. Revealing that the movement's participants were driven by anger and frustration rather than by a shared ideology, the mass media reported that proposals for reducing this inequality ranged from abolishing capitalism to changing tax laws and more vigorous regulation of financial institutions.

Responses to Occupy

Reactions to the movement were predictable, and differed sharply by ideology. Conservatives considered the movement utterly misguided, because increased inequality is the outcome of market forces in capitalism and can be eliminated only by economic growth, which raises incomes for everyone. All of the conservative criticism of the movement echoed the views of two Nobel laureates.

Milton Friedman, arguably one of the most influential economists of the 20th century, stated:

> A society that puts equality – in the sense of equality of outcome – ahead of freedom will end up with neither equality nor freedom. On the other hand, a society that puts freedom first will, as a happy

by-product, end up with both greater freedom and greater equality.[2]

Robert Lucas, widely known as the central figure in the development of the "rational expectation theory", wrote:

Of the tendencies that are harmful to sound economics, the most seductive, and in my opinion the most poisonous, is to focus on questions of distribution. The potential for improving the lives of poor people by finding different ways of distributing current production is nothing compared to the apparently limitless potential of increasing production.[3]

In contrast, many liberals supported the movement, using words consonant with the following views of another two Nobel laureates, Joseph Stiglitz and Paul Krugman. Stiglitz wrote:

The hollowing out of the middle class since the 1970s means that they are unable to invest in their future by educating themselves and their children and by starting or improving businesses. Returns from Wall Street speculation are taxed at a far lower rate than other forms of income. Low tax receipts mean that the government cannot make the vital investments in infrastructure, education, research and health that are crucial for restoring long-term economic strength.[4]

Krugman agreed:

If you take a longer perspective, rising inequality becomes by far the most important single factor behind lagging middle-class incomes. Beyond that, when you try to understand both the Great Recession and the not-so-great recovery that followed, the economic and above all political impacts of inequality loom large.[5]

Thomas Piketty and *Capital in the 21st Century*

The prevalence of discontent with economic inequality and the existing capitalist system is also evident in the steady increase in discussions about these topics in the mass media and in scholarly works. The most famous is a dense, 685-page scholarly tome by Thomas Piketty, a French economist. In his bestseller, *Capital in the 21st Century*, he analyzes a huge amount of data in order to examine the wealth and income distributions of 20 Western economies during the past 250 years.

Many conservative journalists and economists have criticized Piketty's book, but to date none of the criticisms is compelling. Most are essentially quibbles with the data he used and how he has used them, and with his broad definition of "capital" that refers to all forms of wealth. Piketty considers capital to be everything that individuals own that can be transferred or traded through the market. Although this is a much broader definition of capital than is used by most economists, it doesn't affect his historical analyses. And none of the criticisms relating to Piketty's data is substantive, nor do they cast doubt on the essential validity of his analyses. To put it differently, all the criticisms to date are very similar to denials of the anthropogenic causes of climate change – that is, the criticisms of Piketty's data and analysis are based on ideology or economic self-interest.

The conclusion of Piketty's book is useful to better understand the reason for the currently increasing inequality in the distribution of wealth in the developed economies. Piketty's view is that capitalism, based on private property and markets, can be very beneficial to society because it diffuses knowledge and skills that are important in helping an economy grow. But capitalism can also have detrimental effects because it tends to threaten democracy and social justice. The detrimental aspects of capitalism result because, as observed in the historical data for long periods of time, r, the rate of profit and the rental rate of capital (a price charged for the use of property for a specific period), can be significantly higher than g, the rate of growth of income and output.

The inequality $r > g$ implies that wealth accumulated in the past grows more rapidly than output and wages. This inequality expresses a fundamental logical contradiction. The entrepreneur inevitably tends to become a *rentier*, more and more dominant over those who own nothing but their labor. Once constituted, capital reproduces itself faster than output increases. The past devours the future.

The consequences for the long-term dynamics of the wealth distribution are potentially terrifying, especially when one adds that the return on capital varies directly with the size of the initial stake and that the divergence in the wealth distribution is occurring on a global scale. (p. 571)

(In French, *rentier* is defined as "a person who lives on income from properties and/or securities.")

It is important to emphasize that Piketty is describing historical facts and the reason for them, which he has deduced after analyzing all the enormous quantities of data he collected. Thus, criticisms by conservative pundits and economists that his analyses and findings are motivated by political ideology are incorrect. Piketty does suggest a wealth tax as a means to reduce the inequality in distribution of wealth, as will be discussed in Chapter Twelve, but he scrupulously refrains from any discussion of the politics involved in levying such a tax.

Disparity in income and wealth distribution

Let us now turn to data that establish that the disparity in income and wealth distribution has increased in all of the rich economies since the 1980s, today reaching a level that not only threatens democracy but also seriously compromises the performance of these countries' economies. Further data and observations will be presented in chapters to follow that separately discuss the US, Japan, Germany and other developed economies in the EU, but let us here present an overview of these inequalities.

The US

Measuring disparity by the Gini coefficient

The steady rise of inequality in the distribution of income and wealth in the US since the 1980s can be readily seen in the country's Gini coefficient, which is used by social scientists to measure disparity. The Gini coefficient is a measurement of the distribution of income devised in 1912 by Corrado Gini, an Italian sociologist. It is 0 when everyone is receiving the same amount of income, and 1 if one person is receiving all of the income. Thus, the higher the coefficient, the more unequal the distribution of income. The coefficient can also be used to measure disparity in the distribution of wealth.

The Gini coefficient for income distribution in the US rose steadily and sharply from 0.361 in 1980 to 0.451 in 2008, the last year for which we have reliable data that can be used for international comparisons. The last time income inequality in the United States was so extreme was in 1927, when the coefficient was 0.458. This was at the height of "the Gilded Age," a period known for its excessive disparity in the distribution of income and wealth. This inequality owed significantly to increasingly speculative trading of stocks, which was a major reason for the stock market crash of 1929. The crash marked the onset of the Great Depression of the 1930s.

After the Second World War, income taxes on the wealthy and corporate taxes were increased to pay for the cost of the war. This, combined with increased employment and higher real wages following the war, reduced the Gini coefficient to 0.361 by 1980. But most of the gains in equality have now been replaced by the same excessive income disparity that prevailed during the 1920s. The steady rise of the US's Gini coefficient since the 1980s is due to changes in US tax laws and welfare policies, as well as several other reasons that will be described in detail in Chapter Seven. Today, only the emerging economies, such as Brazil, Mexico and China, have a higher Gini coefficient than the US.

Some statistics on income and wealth distribution

Another and more readily comprehensible way of confirming the rise in income inequality is to look at the following statistics. During the 29 years between 1980 and 2008, the top 1 percent of the American population experienced a 179 percent increase in income; the top quintile, 69 percent; the second quintile, 21 percent; the third quintile, 20 percent; the fourth quintile, only 17 percent; and the fifth quintile, a mere 6 percent. Since these are average figures, there can be little doubt that many people, especially in the last quintile, actually saw their incomes decline. Because of the disparity in the rates of increase in income, the wealth of the richest 1 percent of Americans rose most rapidly. In 1980, a mere 1 percent of the US population held 10 percent of the total wealth of the nation, but by 2008 the richest 1 percent held 23.5 percent of total wealth. This is very close to the disparity that prevailed in 1927, when the top 1 percent of the population held 23.9 percent of total wealth.[6]

Conversely, the number of the poor increased steadily during the same three decades, from around 30 million, or about 13 percent of the total population in 1980, to an estimated 43.5 million in 2008, almost 16 percent of the total population. The definition of "poor" is the one adopted and used consistently by the US government: those living in households with an income below the threshold amount in dollars – calculated by adjusting for the difference over time in the costs of various necessities – that is necessary for "families or individuals to meet the basic needs of healthy living." In other words, families not having "a sufficient income level to provide the food, shelter and clothing needed to preserve health."[7]

Inequalities have continued to increase since 2008. While there was an increase of $5 trillion in the net worth of American households after the Great Recession of 2007–08, *all* of the increase between 2009 and 2011 went to the wealthiest 7 percent of American households, further increasing the already large wealth gap in the US. As the economy pulled out of recession, these 8 million households saw their net worth grow to at least $500,000 by 2011, with a median net worth of $836,033. Also in 2011, the total wealth of this group stood at

$25.4 trillion, up from $19.8 trillion in 2009, or an increase of 28 percent. In contrast, the remaining 93 percent of households experienced a decline of 4 percent in their net worth, to $14.8 trillion for the group as a whole, down from $15.4 trillion.[8]

An important reason why the rich have done so much better is that they are much more heavily invested in the stock market, which rallied during 2010 and 2011, due mainly to the Federal Reserve's ultra-easy monetary policies. Less affluent households have most of their wealth tied up in their homes, and the housing market remained stagnant between 2009 and 2011. As a result, by 2011, the average wealth of the top 7 percent was almost 24 times that of the rest of the population. Only two years earlier, the ratio had been 18 to 1.

The trends noted above are still continuing, as noted in *Forbes* and the *New York Times*:

> While real estate across the US slowly recovers from the collapse of the housing bubble, the super luxury market is currently rivaling, and in some cases even trumping, bubble-era prices. Thanks to a handful of recent record purchases – including a $117.5 million Silicon Valley sale in November 2012 – an increasing number of high-end homeowners are attaching ambitious nine-figure price tags to their digs.[9]

> Flooded with homeless encampments from its freeway underpasses to the chic sidewalks of Venice Beach, municipal officials here declared a public emergency on Tuesday, making Los Angeles the first city in the nation to take such a drastic step in response to its mounting problem with 44,000 street dwellers.[10]

The crisis of the homeless is not limited to Los Angeles. The Department of Housing and Urban Development reported on November 20, 2015 that in 2014 there were 560,000 people in the US "who were living on the streets, in cars, in homeless shelters or in subsidized transitional housing during a one-night national survey in January. Nearly one-fourth were aged 18 or under."

The following conclusion of a study of income tax records in the US by Saez and Zucman aptly summarizes the history and the reality of the economic disparity in the US today.

Wealth inequality, it turns out, has followed a spectacular U-shape evolution over the past 100 years. From the Great Depression in the 1930s through the late 1970s there was a substantial democratization of wealth. The trend then inverted, with the share of total household wealth owned by the top 0.1 percent increasing to 22 percent in 2012 from 7 percent in the late 1970s. The top 0.1 percent includes 160,000 families with total net assets of more than $20 million in 2012.[11]

Japan

The economic "bubble" burst in Japan in 1991. Since then, real wages have continued to stall or even decline for many wage earners as the economy remains mired in a prolonged stagnation. The number of the "working poor," those workers earning per year less than 2,000,000 yen (or about $18,000 when one dollar is equal to around 110 yen) rose from 769,000 to 1,069,000 between 1990 and 2014. Since the 1990s, the OECD has continued to list Japan near the bottom of the pack in statistics showing the percentage of the population living in poverty, which is defined as those having less than half of the median income in each country. According to the OECD data, 15.7 percent of Japanese, or about 20 million out of the total population of 128 million, were living in poverty in 2009. Japan's rate was sixth-worst among the 34 OECD countries, which had an average rate of 11 percent. Japan's rate and ranking among OECD countries remained unchanged in 2011.[12]

The number of households with no savings and no financial assets has also risen. According to the annual surveys by the Ministry of Finance, the number increased from around 5 percent during the 1980s to around 10 percent in the 1990s, and by 2014 it had risen to 24.9 percent. And between 1990 and 2014 the number of households receiving welfare payments for subsistence rose from less than half a million to 2 million.

As might be expected from these facts, the Gini coefficient, calculated after various income transfers were made, rose steadily, from 0.295 in 1991 to 0.323 in 2008. Japan's Gini coefficient in 2008 was higher than the OECD average of 0.316 and second only to that of the US. By the end of the first decade of the new century, Japan could no longer claim that it was a country where "almost everyone is middle class," as had often been proclaimed during the postwar decades of rapid growth from the 1950s through the 1970s.

Declining permanent employment

The main reason for the increase in income inequalities since the 1990s has been the steady erosion of Japan's once-vaunted permanent employment system. Under this system, most employees held a job with a single firm throughout their working years. But as the economy continued to stagnate, more and more firms hired an increasing proportion of their personnel on a non-permanent basis. Non-permanent employees are paid distinctly lower wages, receive few benefits and have no prospect of promotion. However, non-permanent employees are in effect hired on a "permanent" basis through multiple renewals of their short-terms contracts.

Data from the Ministry of Internal Affairs and Communications show that the proportion of non-permanent employees reached 32.8 percent in 2009, continued to rise to 36.1 percent by the end of 2012, to 37.6 percent during 2013, and exceeded 40 percent in 2015. The proportion of non-permanent employment in 2014 was much higher among females, at 52.9 percent, in contrast to 17.9 percent among males. Chapter Eight, on Japan, will present more data and observations on the growth in non-permanent employment, unemployment and under-employment, especially among the young, and on other developments that show why economic inequality has been increasing since the 1990s and why Japan's low unemployment rate is a sham figure.

Germany

The German economy grew very slowly during the 1990s by comparison with the immediate postwar decades, but at the beginning of the new century it began to grow faster than other EU economies. However, this performance was achieved at the cost of a significantly slower rate of increase in real wages than in other eurozone economies, as evidenced by labor's decreasing share of GDP. Labor's share in GDP, defined as wages and salaries, was 71.2 percent in 2002 vis-à-vis the share of capital, defined as profits and rents, which stood at 28.2 percent. However, by 2008 labor's share had declined to 67.2 percent, while capital's had risen to 32.8 percent.[13] The two main reasons for this were the pro-business reform of the labor market between 2003 and 2005, and subsequent pro-investment policies, as will be detailed in Chapter Nine on Germany.

The labor market reform and pro-investment policies resulted in a rise in the Gini coefficient, measured after taxes and transfers, from 0.265 in 2000 to 0.285 in 2005, and then to 0.295 in 2008. The 2000 coefficient was close to the low Scandinavian level, but by 2008 it had crept up to just below the OECD average of 0.300.

An OECD report observed the increasing economic disparity in Germany during the years 2000–08:

> For a long period following the war, income disparity in Germany remained relatively small compared to other countries. Now Germany has nearly reached the OECD average ... the number of households without any earned income increased from 15.2 to 19.4 percent. Currently nearly one fifth of households are dependent on some sort of state benefit – the highest level of all OECD countries. Here once again this figure grew rapidly in Germany, which ranks only behind Hungary and Turkey in this respect.[14]

The same OECD report also commented on income distribution in Germany in 2008:

> In Germany the top ten percent of earners receive on average about eight times as much as the lowest ten percent. The top ten percent control a quarter of gross income. Wealth in Germany is even more unequally distributed. The wealthiest 10 percent possess around half of the country's total assets. The last wealth and poverty report issued by the German government demonstrated that the bottom fifty percent of households possess just two percent of total assets. In the meantime over three million households in Germany are insolvent. Individuals or families obliged to receive counseling on their debts owed an average of 23,000 euro and had an income of less than 900 euros per month.

Numerous studies by DIW (Berlin) (the Deutsche Institut für Wirtschaftsforschung, or German Institute of Economic Research, a leading independent, non-profit research organization), and by many German specialists have noted the increasing disparity in income since the 1990s. The DIW *Report on Income Inequality* published in 2014 stated that, as of March 2013, only 60 percent of Germans remained in "the middle income" group, defined as those whose monthly household income was between 860 and 1,844 euros. At the beginning of this century this figure, adjusted for inflation, was 66 percent. During the same 2000–13 period, the number of households in the low-income group (those earning less than 860 euros) rose from 18 percent to 23 percent. The median income for low-income households was 680 euros in 2000, but by 2013 it had declined to 645 euros. This decline occurred despite the fact that the unemployment rate during the same period declined as a trend.

The DIW report noted that in the spring of 2013, 14 percent of Germans were living in poverty, defined as those households earning less than 60 percent of the median income. At the same time, the number of millionaires had grown steadily since the beginning of the century, and rose rapidly, by some 23 percent, from 2011 to 2013, when it stood at around 430,000, the highest number ever. These facts led the authors of the DIW study to conclude that "these trends have serious implications for the health of the society, because the rising wealth of the country has not led to 'prosperity for all,' the great rallying cry of postwar Germany."

Other developed economies

The US, Japan and Germany are not isolated examples. Four large EU economies – France, the UK, Italy and Spain – serve as further examples of the widening disparity in income that is seen in all developed economies.

Because socialist governments were in power for a long period in both France and Spain, the Gini coefficient for both countries declined somewhat between 1980 and 2012. In France, it went down from 0.298 in 1980 to 0.283 in 2012. In Spain the decline was from 0.362 to 0.347 during the same period. Among the OECD economies, the French coefficient is relatively low and the Spanish relatively high. In contrast, in both the UK and Italy, the Gini coefficient rose during the same 32-year period, in the UK from 0.322 to 0.345 and in Italy from 0.280 to 0.337.

However, even in France and Spain, where the Gini coefficient declined a little, the number of billionaires and millionaires has risen since the 1980s, as it has done in the US, Japan, Germany, the UK and Italy. In the early 1980s, when lists of billionaires were first compiled on the US dollar basis, there were only some 40 billionaires in the world, and none in France or Spain. But by 2013, France had 23 and Spain, 20. And between 1980 and 2013 the number of millionaires increased in France from 102,000 to 280,000 and in Spain from 54,000 to 143,000.[15]

While the number of billionaires and millionaires increased in Spain, in 2012 about 4.6 million Spanish households, or 9.8 percent of the total, were living on incomes of less than 40 percent of the median household income, meeting the World Bank's definition of the poor. Since the median income of Spanish households in 2012 was the equivalent of $47,477, these households were living on $18,190 or less. Even without delving into the cost of daily necessities, it is not difficult to envision how deprived these Spanish families were.

Conclusion

In concluding this chapter, let us ask, "Why hasn't democracy in these countries been able to stop the widening of economic disparity that has been seen from the 1980s on?" Or, "Why couldn't a majority of voters prevent the increasing disparities in income and wealth?"

There are three major reasons, all closely interlinked, which will be further discussed in Chapter Twelve. Briefly, they are the following.

First, the rich, who collectively have had an increasing amount of wealth since the 1980s, are able to use their wealth to influence electoral, legislative and regulatory processes. They do so by making campaign contributions and lobbying, and by making use of personal contacts maintained via the revolving employment door between politicians and the leaders of the largest firms and financial institutions, and also between politicians and high office holders in the bureaucracy.

For more evidence on essentially the same view, readers are invited to peruse a readable article by Martin Gilens and Benjamin Page. The authors analyze over 1,800 different policy initiatives from 1981 to 2002 and argue that economic elites and organized groups representing business interests have had an increasingly substantial impact on US government policies. That is, the US has become non-democratic in the sense that labor unions, other interest groups for average citizens, and voters have come to have less and less influence on economic polices adopted in the US since the 1980s.[16]

Second, it has become much easier for the wealthy and politicians to beguile voters into voting for politicians who support legislation that is against voters' self-interest, for two main reasons: the growing complexities of government programs and their intended and unintended outcomes, and the unprecedented ease of mass communication, which has become increasingly conservative. Among the many examples that will be described in the chapters to follow, the starkest are strong political support for pro-investment fiscal and monetary policies and for "small government," which reduces expenditure on safety nets for the needy.

Third, seeing their own income stagnate while the rich get richer and influence politics, many voters have become despairing of politics and are choosing to "exit" (becoming disengaged from politics and not even voting) instead of exercising "voice" (participating in various political activities and voting). A growing number of voters have "exited" from politics in recent decades, enabling the rich to have more political power.

The data provide evidence of this. In the US, where the voter participation rate in presidential elections since 1980s has hovered between 58 and 62 percent, the rate for the mid-term Congressional elections has shown a downward trend. In 2014 it was only 36.4 percent, the lowest since 1942, when the rate was exceptionally low at 33.9 percent. The voter participation rate in Japan's Lower House elections (the counterpart of the House of Representatives in the US) also shows an unmistakable downward trend since the 1980s, going from the mid-70th percentile to a low of 52.7 percent in 2014. In Germany, the voter participation rate in national elections has declined from a high of around 90 percent in the early 1980s to 71 percent in 2013. In all other rich European democracies (France, the UK, Italy and Spain) the downward trend is also unmistakable. And the voter participation rate by age groups shows that in all rich capitalist democracies the rate for young voters is roughly half that for all voters.

Today's politics have become unaccountable to voters in various ways as examples from the US, Japan and Germany show. This too must be changed as an integral part of changing the existing political–economic system.

SIX

Buckling bridges and crumbling mountains

Introduction

In the new world, pro-investment fiscal and monetary policies are not only ineffective but are also having numerous very serious detrimental effects as was shown in the preceding chapters. The goal of this chapter is to discuss the socially necessary investments that I believe are the only way to reinvigorate the economies and democracy of the developed countries.

The chapter begins with a consideration of safety nets and infrastructural investment as examples of socially necessary investments. Of course, these are not the only necessary investments – others include improving the quality of education from pre-school through university; providing adequate housing and healthcare for all citizens; and supporting needed research in numerous fields such as medicine and the sciences. The chapter's second section stresses the urgency of substantially increasing investment to avert an environmental catastrophe. Although there is already an abundant literature on all of these socially necessary investments, my hope is that what I present here, along with my personal experience, will be useful in supporting the central arguments of this book.

Social safety nets and infrastructural investment

It is an irrefutable fact that social safety nets in the developed economies have become frayed in the past few decades. OECD data collected since the 1980s reveal that total expenditures on safety nets to aid those in need (the poor, the aged, the unemployed and the disabled) as a ratio of GDP have been falling as a trend in *all* of the large developed economies. The only exceptions are the five small Nordic countries of Denmark, Norway, Finland, Sweden and Iceland. This means that while a majority of citizens in the most developed economies have continued to enjoy more and more necessary luxuries since the 1980s, the safety nets have been becoming increasingly deficient.

In 2014, the US, with the highest Gini coefficient, and Japan, with one of the highest, among the developed economies both had a significantly lower ratio of total expenditures for safety nets to GDP than did the developed economies in Europe. While the ratio was 8.0 percent for the US and 9.1 percent for Japan, for the developed European economies the ratios were: Germany, 15.9 percent; France, 17.4; the UK, 13.7; Spain, 13.2; and Italy, 18.7. In other words, the US and Japan, the two countries that have most aggressively pursued pro-investment fiscal and monetary policies, were letting their safety nets fray more than were other developed economies. And they were doing so even as inequalities in income and wealth distribution among their citizens continued to widen.

The neglect of infrastructural investment by the developed economies is no less stark. OECD data and numerous studies leave no doubt that the developed economies have been investing a decreasing proportion of their GDP in maintaining and upgrading their infrastructures, at the cost of economic efficiency and the quality of life. For example, in the US, infrastructural expenditures, including those relating to transportation (such as roads, airports, bridges, levees, dams and harbors), declined from an average of 3.8 percent of GDP during the period 1960–80 to only 2.4 percent by the early 2010s.

Not surprisingly, such a decline in investment has had numerous and increasingly serious consequences.

America once had the best road and transportation system in the world, but nothing lasts forever. Last May [2014], the I-5 bridge near Seattle buckled when an overloaded tractor trailer grazed an overhead girder, sending two cars plummeting into the river below. In 2007, a stretch of the I-35W bridge in Minneapolis collapsed during rush hour, killing 13, injuring 145, and resulting in repairs costing $234 million. Throughout the country, many urban roads and highways built decades ago now carry five to ten times the traffic the original engineers expected and require constant emergency repair creating horrible traffic jams. Water and gas pipelines laid in the first half of the 20th century are failing, leading to explosions and floods. "Some of this infrastructure is more than 100 years old," said Rick Grant, owner of a Maryland structural engineering firm, "but it wasn't designed with more than a 50-year life span in mind."[1]

Other countries show a similar decline in investment in their infrastructures. For Japan, total investment in infrastructure as a percentage of GDP has fallen from between 5.8 and 6.4 percent in the 1960s to between 3.0 and 3.4 percent during the 2010s. For Germany, the decline was from around 3.8 percent to below 2 percent during the same period. OECD data show that in most other developed economies, including Sweden (but not the other Nordic countries), the trend of decline is very similar.

All of these declines justify the following observations.

The US needs 3.6 trillion dollars in infrastructure investments to bring the current overall grade from D+ because America's transportation infrastructure is quickly falling behind the rest of the world as roads continue to fall into disrepair, railroad lines age, and airports become more congested resulting in longer commute times.[2]

Today, Japan's infrastructure investment is much less than it was 30 years ago. To prevent the further decline of its economy, investment must be increased immediately and significantly, even if it means selling more government bonds.[3]

Germany has long had a reputation for excellent infrastructure. But in recent years both public and private investment has declined dramatically.[4]

Germany is living off its reserves. Bridges are crumbling and universities are deteriorating, and not enough is being spent to maintain phone networks. All of Germany's political parties pledged to spend more money on highways, transportation and education during the upcoming legislative period – but they have often made such promises in the past. In the end, however, the already meager budgets for investment were slashed. It will be a similar story this time around.[5]

In sum, while the trend since the 1980s has been to reduce taxes on income and corporations in order to continue ineffective pro-investment policies, the proportion of total government expenditure on safety nets and infrastructure has been decreasing in all large economies, and has not been rising even in the Nordic countries.

The crumbling Eiger

The urgency of the need to increase investment to prevent further degradation of the environment was brought home to me on a visit to Switzerland. In July 2006, my wife and I were staying at a hotel in Grindelwald, an alpine village southwest of Bern and located under the famous North Face of the Eiger and its glacier. Our hotel was approximately three kilometers across the valley from the mountain.

One morning, shortly after dawn, we were awoken by thunderous noises coming from the direction of the Eiger. Startled, we looked toward the mountain and saw a huge, grey dust cloud rising high into the sky from the edge of the mountain next to the glacier's path. Tons of rock, including gigantic boulders, along with an immense quantity of gravel and dirt, were cascading down toward the river valley. In no time, the dust cloud drifted over the village, obscuring the houses. The noise and the avalanche of rocks and dirt gradually stopped and, as the dust cloud dissipated, we could see that a stalagmite-like rock column as high as the Empire State building that once stood at the edge of Eiger was gone forever.

By the end of the day, we learned that the accelerating pace of melting of the glacier, which had supported the eastern flank of the mountain, was the cause of the huge rockslides that had been occurring every few years since the 1990s. As the ice retreated, the side of the mountain was crumbling. Estimates of the amount of rock, gravel and dirt that had fallen into the valley varied, but the lowest were several hundred thousand cubic meters. The melting of the same glacier had caused a lake to form under the ice, necessitating the expenditure of millions of francs in subsequent years to drain the lake in order to prevent it from bursting and inundating the valley and the village.

Average temperatures in Switzerland have been rising by more than half a degree Celsius on average every decade since 1970, resulting in an 18 percent loss of the surface of glaciers between 1985 and 2000. For us, it was a case of "seeing is believing." With our own eyes we had seen that the climate was warming dangerously and the world now faced a crisis unprecedented in recorded history.

Given my experience, I readily understood the message of Kenneth Chang's article "The Big Melt Accelerates", which appeared in the *New York Times* on May 19, 2014.

> Centuries from now, a large swath of the West Antarctic ice sheet is likely to be gone, its hundreds of trillions of tons of ice melted, causing a four-foot

rise in already swollen seas. Scientists reported last week that the scenario may be inevitable, with new research concluding that some giant glaciers had passed the tipping point of no return, possibly setting off a chain reaction that could doom the rest of the ice sheet. For many, the research signaled that changes in the earth's climate have already reached a tipping point, even if global warming halted immediately.

Nothing but a major global effort

An environmental catastrophe cannot be averted if a major international effort is not begun immediately. This is the conclusion reported in the 6,000-pages-long, the *Fifth Assessment Report* of the IPCC (Intergovernmental Panel on Climate Change of the UN), compiled by 800 of the world's top scientists and other experts and published in 2014. In order to avoid a 2°C increase in temperature – the level above which catastrophic damage will occur – global emissions must be reduced to half their current level by 2050. Unless all countries make a strong commitment to reduce carbon emissions immediately, the world's environment will pass the tipping point and suffer the irredeemable consequences of doing too little too late.

If no major global effort to reduce carbon emissions is made in the very near future, at least 177 million people – mostly in Asia (about 50 million of them in China) – will experience frequent floods by the end of this century. This is in addition to the large number of people living in low-lying countries and in island nations, such as the Netherlands, Bangladesh and the Maldives, which are already seeing increasingly frequent flooding. But flooding is occurring in other countries as well, such as in the UK and along the Mississippi River in the US[6]

Flooding not only endangers lives but also has very high economic costs. For example, a group of Harvard scholars estimated that "rising seas could put American property worth 66 to 106 billion dollars literally under water by 2050" and noted that "If the numbers are any guide, the real damage would be greater still."[7] And, as an increasing number of news reports make us aware, droughts have been becoming longer and more severe worldwide in recent decades. These droughts are imposing an increasing economic cost and endangering the lives of more and more people because they reduce the water available for drinking, agriculture and many other uses and increase the frequency of large-scale forest fires.

Noting these developments, Antonio Guterres, the former UN High Commissioner of Refugees, stressed that all the world's countries in must be concerned with "the case of entire populations forced to migrate due to the lack of access to clean water, productive land or the occurrence of natural disasters." He went on to say:

> Climate change further exacerbates this issue through drought and desertification, two of the major factors contributing to food insecurity because they render land unsuitable for agriculture. Without productive lands, farmers cannot grow crops and are forced to leave their land plots in search of more fertile territories, which often cross national boundaries. Currently, over 1.5 billion people depend on degrading land and more than 1 billion are experiencing droughts. Climate change will exacerbate these issues, and most likely increase the number of environmental refugees, presently surpassing 36 million worldwide.[8]

Despite Guterres' assessment and the data and findings of the IPCC, the developed economies continue to do far less than is necessary to try to avert a catastrophe. To be sure, many governments have adopted numerous policies because those who are working towards doing more to sustain the environment have won some victories in policymaking arenas and in the courts. A good example is the US Supreme Court case in which in June 2014 the Environmental Protection Agency won the right to regulate greenhouse gases emitted by modified utility plants. However, the victory, won on a 7 to 2 decision, was restrained in that, in a separate 5 to 4 vote, the Court rejected the Agency's broad assertion of regulatory power under one section of the Clean Air Act.

As the continuing climate warming demonstrates, such victories in the developed economies have been too few to reverse the tide, despite the fact that in the battle against the looming environmental tipping point the developed economies must take a lion's share of the responsibility. This is because today's developed economies are the economies that have been emitting greenhouse gases and polluting the air since they began to industrialize, as the following quotation reminds us.

> A London fog is brown, reddish-yellow, or greenish, darkens more than a white fog, has a smoky, or sulfurous smell, is often somewhat dryer than a country fog, and produces, when thick, a choking sensation. Instead of diminishing while the sun rises higher, it often increases in density, and some of the most lowering London fogs occur about midday or late in the afternoon. Sometimes the brown masses rise and interpose a thick curtain at a considerable elevation between earth and sky. A white cloth spread out on the ground rapidly turns dirty, and particles of soot attach themselves to every exposed object.[9]

Carbon dioxide (CO_2) emissions *per person* measured in tons in 2012 were: 16.4 for the US; 10.4 for Japan; 9.7 for Germany; 7.7 for the UK; 7.1 for China; and 1.6 for India, according to estimates made in 2013 by the European Commission. In short, the developed economies are responsible for the environmental crisis we are facing today.

Effective policies on emissions

Although developing economies such as China and India that have now become major emitters of greenhouse gases must do their best to limit their emissions, the fact remains that the developed economies must do what is necessary to prevent the looming environmental tipping point. The critical question is this: why haven't policies sufficient to reduce and reverse the trend of environmental degradation, especially the critical emission of carbon dioxide, already been adopted by the developed economies?

The answer is that many politicians, business leaders and voters believe their political power, their profits or their incomes would be negatively affected by more robust environmental policies. Their shortsightedness is preventing the adoption of the policies that are necessary to prevent the coming of the tipping point within the next few decades. What has created this regrettable outcome is the strength of misguided arguments such as the following:

1. None of the results of scientific research to date has convincingly demonstrated that human actions have been responsible for climate warming and other environment degradation. Rather, this is a natural phenomenon out of our control. Thus there is little reason to allocate more resources to protect the environment, at the cost of economic growth.

2. Scientific studies presumably showing the urgency of the need to do more to protect the environment are an elaborate hoax put forth by the liberals. Whatever the scientific findings, doing more to protect the environment means more government involvement. This would reduce the efficient working of capitalism, which is indispensable for economic growth.

3. Since the developing economies, such as China and India, are causing environmental problems at such a rapid pace and of such huge magnitude, there is no reason for the developed economies to do more, to the detriment of their own economic performance.

Argument 1 is feigned skepticism or ignorant anti-scientism, put forth despite overwhelming scientific evidence to the contrary. This is the same brazen deception as was used at a US Congressional hearing in April of 1994 by the seven CEOs of the largest American cigarette firms when they all denied that nicotine is addictive.

Argument 2 is no more than a desperate ruse motivated by ideology and/or political or financial gain. The "efficient working of capitalism" is a fig-leaf to conceal shortsighted self-interest.

Argument 3 is ludicrous because the developed economies, which polluted and degraded the environment freely from the time they began to industrialize until only several decades ago, are still the major emitters of pollution. This argument also ignores the fact that today the per capita consumption of energy from fossil fuel and other sources and the consequent emissions per capita in the developed economies are at least 10 to 100 times greater than the energy consumption and emissions output in all of the emerging economies.[10]

The IPCC's Fifth Assessment Report and the Paris Agreement of 2015

In 2014 the *Fifth Assessment Report* of the IPCC, cited above, reported that the reductions in emissions that were necessary to avert the environmental tipping point would require huge investments. The Assessment describes the mitigation scenarios needed to make improvements in the technology of energy production from fossil fuels and renewables in order to stabilize atmospheric greenhouse gas concentrations in the range of 430–530 ppm CO_2eq (parts per million, CO_2 equivalent) by 2100. They would require an additional annual global investment of about $177 billion through 2029. Further, the annual incremental investment necessary globally to improve energy-use efficiency (involving the modernization of existing equipment and infrastructures) must increase by about $336 billion per year, also until 2029. The total comes to $513 billion per annum over a 15-year period, on top of the annual investments that the developed economies have been making during recent years.[11]

A very large proportion of this additional annual investment of $513 billion must be made collectively by the developed economies. If their existing capitalist system remains unchanged and they continue to follow their current fiscal and monetary policies, they will not be able to make the investment necessary to avert the environmental tipping point and at the same time create the increased demand that will enable their economies to grow.

A meeting to discuss the global environmental crisis was held by the United Nations in Paris from November 20 to December 11, 2015 and was attended by the political leaders and scientists of 196 countries. Its purpose was essentially to adopt the recommendations of the *Fifth Assessment Report* of the IPCC. Most news reports called this a major victory in our efforts to prevent further degradation of the environment. However, as was expected, the outcome was in fact only another victory in a skirmish, and the war is far from won. This is evident in the principal agreement reached. Each country has promised to reduce its greenhouse gas emissions in order to prevent a global temperature rise by 2°C (possibly 1.5°C), but the agreement is to be implemented on the "honor" system, with no international enforcement. The developed economies are to provide at least $100 billion per year, starting in 2020, to aid the developing economies in their efforts to reduce emissions. And the agreement is to be effective only if 55 countries, or the countries emitting 55 percent of the total emissions, ratify the agreement.

Unfortunately, there are numerous reasons why the Paris Agreement is only a victory in a skirmish, one that is certain to be followed by many more skirmishes. The "pledged" contributions towards the $100 billion to be paid by the developed economies include a contribution from the US of at least $10 billion annually. That this pledge will be honored is highly problematic because it is very likely that the Republican Party, whose leaders have already voiced strong opposition to the Agreement, will continue to control the House of Representatives. To be sure, more and more American voters have become highly concerned about the sustainability of their environment. But to believe that the US Congress will ratify the Agreement and continue to provide at least $10 billion per year over the coming decades is simply not realistic. And this is not the situation just in the US. It would be naïve to believe that all the other developed economies will be able to honor their pledges over the coming years.

Conclusion

For those of us who are very concerned about the future of our environment, the Paris Agreement is another triumph in the ongoing political skirmishes. However, in order to the triumph meaningful, we must first change the existing capitalist system, because that is the only way to put an end to ineffective pro-investment policies and to reinvigorate our economies by increasing investments to meet societal needs. And the most important societal need of all is to increase investments to avert further degradation of the environment.

SEVEN

The United States: stagnation and gridlock

American politics has suffered increasing paralysis since the 1980s as the economy has stagnated and disparity in the distribution of income and wealth has grown. This chapter discusses developments from the 1980s to the present in two sections, the first from 1981 until the end of the Great Recession of 2007–08, and the second from the beginning of the Obama administration.

From Ronald Reagan to George W. Bush, 1981–2009

With the election of Ronald Reagan in 1980, politics in the United States made a significant shift to the Right. This shift continued with Reagan's Republican Party successors, George H.W. Bush and his son George W. Bush. Even the Democratic president, William J. Clinton, was significantly more conservative than other post-Second World War presidents of his own party.

Broadly stated, the shift to the Right took place largely because of the reaction of voters to the trends of decline in the economic growth rate and in real incomes, both of which were becoming evident by the end of the 1970s. The growth rate of the economy was 5.5 percent in 1977 but fell to 1.4 percent in 1979 and rebounded only slightly, to 2.7 percent in 1980. Thus, by the beginning of the 1980s, American voters faced the two realities noted in Chapter One: the growth rates both of the economy and of real wages were slowing. In the case of the US this was due to the slowed growth of labor productivity, rapid inflation and the oil crises of 1974 and 1979. Moreover, a majority of citizens had entered a new world in which they had become sated with the necessities of life and were enjoying more necessary luxuries. To increase their real incomes and enable them to enjoy even more necessary luxuries, a growing number of Americans welcomed the rightward shift in politics that promised both while at the same time reducing their taxes.

A brief history of technological change

Another very important reason for the ideological shift to the Right both in the US and in other developed economies during the late 20th century was a historic technological change that began during the 1970s. This may seem like a digression, but it is necessary to discuss in order to understand the shift to conservative politics.

This historic change is known as the Information Technology (IT) Revolution. Historical analysis shows that a major ideological shift to the Right also occurred during the early phase of similar historic technological changes that occurred in the UK and in the US. In order to show that the IT Revolution, which began in the 1970s, was especially important in shifting American politics to the Right during the 1980s, let's briefly examine the ideological shifts that occurred during the early phases of two previous historic technological changes.[1]

A study of economic history from the beginning of the Industrial Revolution reveals that there have been three waves of technological change since the 18th century. The first began in England during the 1760s and the second, led by the US, began during the 1880s. The US also led the third wave, which began during the 1970s and is still ongoing.

The Industrial Revolution

The first wave of change began when the innovation of the steam engine replaced human and animal energy as the main source of power. The rapidly increasing use of steam-powered textile and other machines, as well as steamships, transformed the English economy. Throughout this first wave, the volume of international trade rose rapidly, due to the invention of steamships and the steadily rising output of cotton textile and other industrial products. Enriched by all the fruits of technological change, England increased its military might, led by its navy, and expanded its global empire.

During the first three decades of the first technological revolution the organization of business changed fundamentally. The most significant change was the emergence of companies owned by shareholders, which enabled firms to obtain the large amounts of capital necessary to manufacture and market new products. Shareholders were people who shared risks and profits, replacing the traditional suppliers of capital – rich noblemen and merchants. Companies that were hugely profitable, thanks to the new technology, became oligopolists. They comprised the small number of first entrants into a market who managed to capture a large share of the market, thus earning large profits. As the political power of industrial firms expanded, with the oligopolists at the forefront, business leaders and investors emerged as the *nouveaux riches* and succeeded in steadily changing the tax, labor and other laws for their own benefit. The result was to make life dismal for industrial workers.

The second wave of change

In the 1880s, a second wave of technological change began. This wave was characterized by the sharply increasing use of petroleum, electricity and steel, the expansion of the mass production method and the appearance of countless synthetic chemical products such as rubber and dyes, and many other developments. The leader of this new wave was the US, which pioneered the generation of electricity, the development of the petroleum industry and the mass production of many industrial products, including automobiles. A continuing inflow of a large number of immigrants assured the US of an adequate supply of labor at low wages.

Just as had occurred during the first wave, industrial financing changed dramatically and steadily during the first few decades of the second wave. Because of much larger requirements for capital, compared to during the first few decades of the Industrial Revolution, stock markets became much more important and some banks, the providers of capital, grew extremely large, dominating financial markets. In the second wave too, business leaders came to exert enormous influence on American politics in order to ensure the election of their favored candidates and thereby stifle labor movements so as to minimize the cost of labor. What constraints had existed hitherto on the anti-competitive behavior of oligopolistic and monopolistic firms were weakened. In short, American politics shifted to the Right at the cost of widening the inequality in the distribution of income and wealth.

The IT Revolution

The third wave of technological change was led by the rapid development of IT during the 1970s, with the output of computer chips increasing exponentially starting in 1975. The practical use of computers by both firms and individuals spread rapidly, making the 1980s the first of approximately three decades of rapid change in how business obtained capital. Large IT-related firms, most of which early on began to do business internationally, required even larger amounts of capital and fewer constraints on their market activities than had large firms in the second wave of change. Thus, these IT firms, along with the large financial institutions that were providing an increased amount of capital to the IT and related industries, were strongly motivated to have a pro-business government: a government that imposed fewer taxes and was willing to reduce regulations. They found their demands increasingly met as American politics shifted to the Right during the first 30 years of the third wave, which included the Democratic Clinton administration during the 1990s.

Stagflation in the late 1970s

By the end of the 1970s, the same decade that IT development was beginning to accelerate, President Jimmy Carter was forced to implement a deficit-financed fiscal policy to stimulate demand in order to maintain the economic growth rate and reduce the unemployment rate, which ranged between 5.9 and 7.1 percent. However, this policy failed. Instead, it raised the inflation rate from 6.5 percent in 1977 to 13.5 percent by 1980, bringing about what the mass media called "stagflation," that is, economic stagnation combined with inflation.

The stagflation of the late 1970s occurred for many reasons, including the decreasing international competitiveness of American manufacturing industries, the oil crises and a sustained low interest rate policy by the Fed. But the major reason was that demand was starting to grow only slowly during the decade, despite the deficit-financed fiscal policy and the Fed's easy money policy. The US was in the vanguard of the world's developed economies as they entered the new world of necessary luxuries. This is strongly alluded to in the well-known "Crisis of Confidence" speech that President Carter made on July 15, 1979:

> In a nation that was proud of hard work, strong families, close-knit communities, and our faith in God, too many of us now tend to worship self-indulgence and consumption. Human identity is no longer defined by what one does, but by what one owns. But we've discovered that owning things and consuming things does not satisfy our longing for meaning.

Small government

Because of the voters' reaction to the slowed economic growth and the beginning of the third wave of technological change, Reagan won the 1980 election by promising a "small government," meaning one that would reduce taxes and regulations: actions that it was claimed would reinvigorate the economy. But the consequences of the Reagan policies based on supply-side economics were continued slow growth, a larger national debt, a widening disparity in income and wealth and diminished attention to socially necessary investment. Nevertheless, the shift to the Right remained. Reagan was re-elected and then succeeded by his vice president, George H.W. Bush (1989–93), who also followed the conservative policy line.

With the economy continuing to grow slowly, a Democrat, William J. Clinton, was elected in 1992 and re-elected in 1996, thus serving as president from 1993 to 2001. Clinton did not accept the conservative mantra of small government. Nevertheless, he followed the conservative policy line of "less government," as evidenced in his supporting and signing the Gramm-Leach-Bliley Act (1999), the Commodity Futures Modernization Act (2000) and the Personal Responsibility and Work Opportunity Reconciliation Act (1996) into law.

The Gramm-Leach-Bliley Act nullified the Glass–Steagall Act of 1933, which had prohibited commercial banks from engaging in investment banking. This was the profitable but risky investment activity that used depositors' money and was one of the principal causes of the bankruptcies of so many banks during the 1930s. Nullification of this Act made it possible for large banks to once again engage in investment activities using both their own money (proprietary capital) plus borrowed funds in order to earn large profits. By the eve of the financial crisis of 2007–08, some of the largest banks and financial institutions had a leverage ratio – the ratio of borrowed capital to proprietary funds – of as high as 30. Such a high ratio, leading the largest financial institutions to take unwarranted risks, was one of the main reasons for the financial crisis that sparked the Great Recession of 2007–08, which necessitated a taxpayer bailout of many large financial institutions.

The Commodity Futures Modernization Act of 2000 was the second significant law enacted under the Clinton administration that involved financial institutions. This Act legalized over-the-counter trading of derivatives (financial instruments used to hedge risks and to engage in highly speculative activities). The third law, the Personal Responsibility and Work Opportunity Reconciliation Act of 1996, shifted most of the costs of welfare programs to the states and limited benefits to two consecutive years, with a lifetime limit of five years. This Act put an end to the much more lenient provision of welfare that had been in effect since the Great Depression.

Although he failed to win a majority of the popular vote, the Republican candidate, George W. Bush, became president in 2001 and was re-elected by winning 50.7 percent of the total votes in 2004. During his administration (2001–09), two major laws were enacted to reduce taxes. The Economic Growth and Tax Relief Reconciliation Act of 2001 reduced both income tax rates and taxes on estates and gifts. The Jobs and Growth Tax Relief Reconciliation Act of 2003 accelerated the planned phase-in of the tax cuts under the 2001 law and reduced taxes on income from dividends and capital gains.

Under the 2001 Act, the tax on capital gains and dividends was fixed at 15 percent and levied separately from all other income. This benefited high-income earners who owned disproportionately large amounts of stocks, bonds and properties. For example, the Statistical Abstract of the US Census reported that the wealthiest 5 percent of Americans owned around 60 percent of all individually held stocks in 2009. The tax cuts made the US tax rates the lowest among all 34 OECD countries.

Although the following relates to the Obama years, we should add here that the Bush tax laws had sunset provisions and were due to expire in 2010. However, they were extended for a further two years under the Obama administration through the Tax Relief, Unemployment Insurance Reauthorization and Job Creation Act of 2010. And then the Taxpayer Relief Act of 2012 eliminated the sunset provisions, thus maintaining the tax rate of 15 percent on capital gains and dividends and continuing the reduced tax rates for the higher-income earners. The exception was for couples earning over $450,000 and filing a joint tax return and individuals earning over $225,000, who were required to pay income tax at the pre-Bush higher rates.

Contrary to claims by the supporters of supply-side economics, the Bush tax cuts, which were intended to increase the supply of capital for investment, did not help the economy to grow faster. As discussed in Chapter One, this was mainly because more investment was not needed when demand was increasing slowly and excess productive capacity existed in most industries. The national debt did not decline. Instead, it rose steadily during the Reagan and George W. Bush administrations. This was not only because the slow economic growth did not increase tax revenues, but also because Reagan steadily increased expenditures for national defense.

During the two decades when the Federal Reserve Bank was under the leadership of Alan Greenspan, a devotee of supply-side economics, the Fed aggressively pursued an easy money policy. During his tenure as chairman (1987–2006), he pursued a sustained low interest-rate policy in order to try to increase the growth rate of the economy and mitigate the effects of the bursting of the dot.com bubble in 2000. The bubble occurred because the stock prices of hi-tech firms in the IT sector and other closely related industries had risen too rapidly as a result of overly sanguine investment.

Also during the Greenspan years, and as referred to above, financial institutions, especially the largest banks and hedge funds, took advantage of the steadily decreasing interest rates and engaged in an increasingly large amount of risky but highly profitable activities, most of which had become possible because of the passage of the Gramm-Leach-Bliley Act and the Commodity Futures Modernization Act during the Clinton administration.

The Great Recession

The Great Recession that began in the US in 2007 had numerous causes. Among the most important were: (1) the Federal Reserve Bank's low interest rate policy and its lax oversight of the Securities and Exchange Commission and other governmental agencies that were supposed to monitor and regulate the activities of financial institutions; (2) the passage of the two Acts noted above, which allowed risky financial trading; and (3) the deterioration of ethical standards in financial institutions and among participants in the financial market.

The effects of the recession quickly reverberated around the world, triggering similar financial crises and severe recessions with devastating consequences in Ireland, Greece, Portugal and Spain, and in many other parts of the world as well. But the effects were most immediate in the US, which fell into its severest economic crisis since the Great Depression of the 1930s. In 2008, the stock market tumbled 34 percent and 8.4 million jobs were lost, raising the unemployment rate to 10 percent. At the epicenter of the financial crisis was Lehman Brothers, a global financial firm founded in 1850 and holding over $600 billion in assets when it went bankrupt in September 2008. The bankruptcy resulted because the firm could not get the cash necessary to meet its daily obligations in a paralyzed financial market and could not get assistance from the Treasury Department, which had no authority to help firms, prior to the enactment of the Emergency Economic Stabilization Act. This law authorized the Treasury Department to "bail out" firms, but was not enacted by Congress until October 2008.

The Emergency Economic Stabilization Act provided $700 billion to enable the Treasury Department and the Fed to bail out financial institutions. While the Treasury bailed out several of largest financial institutions, the Fed purchased mortgage-backed securities and other distressed financial assets and supplied cash directly to banks and other financial institutions.

The Federal Reserve Bank, under its new chairman, Ben Bernanke (2006–14), reacted swiftly to try to prevent a systemic collapse of financial institutions. During late 2008, the Fed made nearly $1 trillion of credit available to financial institutions by adopting various unorthodox measures, as well as cutting the federal fund rate for uncollateralized, short-term loans from 5.25 percent to virtually zero. Despite these measures, the crisis continued to deepen, threatening a systemic failure of financial institutions.

Since tax revenues were plummeting, due to the tax cuts in 2001 and 2003 and the slumping economy, and also because of the ballooning cost of the Iraq War, the national debt stood at $10.024 trillion when Bush left office in 2009. This was in marked contrast to the $5.674 trillion debt when he assumed office in 2001. The national debt to GDP ratio of 74 percent of GDP in 2008 was far higher than the 40 percent during the Great Depression of the 1930s. As a result, in 2011 the US lost

Standard & Poor's AAA rating of its bonds for the first time in the 70-year history of Standard & Poor's rating of government bonds.

Societal problems and ideological conflict

As American politics shifted to the Right, the potential for "vertical economic mobility" declined substantially from the 1980s to 2008. This mobility is defined as the possibility for children born to poor families to move up the income ladder. According to the Federal Reserve Bank of Boston, by 2008 vertical mobility had become as limited as in the UK, known for its long-standing disparities in the distribution of income and wealth. It was also lower than in France, a country well known for its lack of vertical mobility. As many as 50 percent of the children of the poor in the US remained poor, in comparison to 41 percent in France and 15 percent in Denmark. And a disproportionately high percentage of those in the bottom quintile are black, highlighting the racial inequality that persists in the US.[2] By the beginning of the 21st century, it had become apparent that "the American dream" – that anyone can climb the income ladder to "success" – was illusive for a rapidly increasing number of Americans.

Among many other indicators of societal problems closely related to the increasing Gini coefficient, decreasing vertical mobility and other persisting consequences of sluggish economic performance is the high incarceration rate in the US. The number of people in US prisons today is the highest in the world. As of 2013, 698 per 100,000 people were incarcerated in federal, state, local and military prisons. In comparison, the same ratio in Russia, which had the second-highest incarceration rate, stood at 577. In China, the ratio was 120 and in Canada, 117. The US population has about 5 percent of the world's population, but in 2013 it had nearly one-quarter of the entire world's prison inmates, at nearly 3.2 million.[3] The economic and social costs of imprisoning so many of its citizens are incalculable.

As the rightward shift in politics and stagnation of the economy continued from 1980 on, ideological conflicts intensified. By the mid-1990s, politics had become gridlocked, as exemplified in the government shutdowns that "furloughed" a large majority of employees of the federal government and suspended all non-essential services for a total of 27 days during two periods in December 1995 and January 1996. The shutdown was due to the inability of Clinton and the Republican-controlled Congress to agree on the government budget and raising the national debt limit.

The general election in November of 2008 was held in "a perfect storm" of the Great Recession, intense discontent with a Republican president who had waged a war of choice in Iraq and a formidable Democratic candidate.

The Obama years, 2009–16

President Barack Obama was inaugurated at one of the most challenging economic times in American history. His administration had to find a way to revive an economy that could spiral deeper into a prolonged depression like that of the 1930s. Thanks to the fact that the Democratic Party controlled both the House and the Senate during the first two years of the new administration, within two months of Obama's taking office, it succeeded in enacting the American Recovery and Reinvestment Act of 2009, or simply the Recovery Act. This $787 billion stimulus package provided funding for education, health, energy efficiency and renewable energies, homeland security and law enforcement and scientific research. The Act also included various measures to strengthen unemployment benefits and help low-income workers, along with various grants to the states. It was also an effort to stimulate the economy by offsetting the decline in private spending with greater public spending. The Act was passed largely on party lines, with only a handful of Republicans in both the House and Senate voting for it.

Despite these new policies, the quarterly economic growth rates in 2009 were dismal: -3.3, -4.2, -4.6 and -3.3 percent. The unemployment rate remained at close to 10 percent – a level not seen since the recession of the early 1980s, which had resulted from a sudden contraction of the money supply by the Federal Reserve Bank's trying to tame the Carter-era double-digit inflation. The worsening economic conditions under the new Obama administration intensified the arguments between the supporters of supply-side economics and those urging even larger deficit-financed government expenditures. Defying logic and ignoring the sequence of events, Republicans and other supporters of supply-side economics argued that the deep recession was being perpetuated by the "big government" and "socialistic" tax-and-spend policies of the Obama administration. In their argument, they lumped together the $700 billion spent bailing out the financial institutions and the $787 billion spent under the American Recovery and Reinvestment Act, even though the financial bailout had been initiated by the Bush administration. They maintained that the economic fortunes of all Americans could be improved only by adopting the Republican policy of small government, which would reduce taxes and minimize regulations on business.

The Tea Party movement

No group has pushed the argument for small government more vociferously than the Tea Party movement, a network of loosely organized local political groups. They took their name from the Boston Tea Party, organized in 1773 to oppose the imposition of a tax on tea by the British government. Its members tend to support the Republican Party but are far more adamant than mainstream Republicans in their support of small government. They have remained strongly opposed to the American Recovery and Reinvestment Act.

According to a CBS-*New York Times* poll conducted in August 2010, the movement's main supporters tend to be white, married, middle-aged and older men who consider themselves conservative and usually vote Republican. Although the results of this and other polls, based on limited numbers of respondents, are only indicative, the average income of people in the movement is higher than the average US household income. However, many independents and some disgruntled Democrats have joined the movement. Polls put the number of

Democratic members of the Tea Party at somewhere between 4 and 15 percent.

Obamacare

Despite strong opposition from the Republicans and the Tea Party, the Patient Protection and Affordable Care Act was enacted in March 2010 on a party-line vote by the Democrats, who controlled both the House and Senate. The major goal of the Act was to enable the nearly 48 million uninsured Americans to obtain health insurance. In all rich democracies, except in the US, universal or near-universal healthcare is the norm, with all or part financed by the government. Thus, for President Obama this legislation was a signature policy, one that could help to define his legacy.

It is difficult to overemphasize the historic importance of the passage of what came to be known by both his supporters and his critics as Obamacare. Strong Republican and Tea Party opposition argued that the Act would lead to a large and costly government policy that would push government deficits even higher. This was the reason why Obamacare was designed to provide a uniquely American healthcare insurance system, necessitated by the ideological divide in the nation. It provides a complex, multi-layered system that involves insurance companies, state government and a nationally administered "exchange" system under which individuals can choose an insurance policy. The Act enables individuals to choose their own insurance plans and also provides subsidies to those who are unable to afford health insurance.

Obamacare is still strongly opposed by Republicans and Tea Party members who ignore or wilfully misinterpret facts that are all too evident to objective observers. To note only the most important benefit of Obamacare, at least 13.4 million people had obtained health insurance for the first time by the end of 2014. Although the exact proportions of those newly signed up for Obamacare care and those renewing their Obamacare insurance were not given, the government announced in December 2015 that "a total of more than 8.5 million people have signed up for Obamacare during 2015."[4]

The cost of premiums did not soar as many Republican politicians had predicted. Instead, it declined by 4 percent in 2014.[5] In addition, "the quality of health care data is improving exponentially. Pressures to reduce costs are ratcheting up. Profitable niches are growing for efficiency improving products."[6] In short, Obamacare has done what it was intended to do: to provide affordable healthcare to as many Americans as possible who had not been able to obtain health insurance because they were poor, unemployed or had a pre-existing medical condition. There is little doubt that a large majority of those who still oppose Obamacare do not understand the complex law and are parroting the criticisms propounded by conservative politicians and pundits.

Legislative gridlock

In the biennial congressional election of November 2010, the Democrats barely succeeded in retaining the Senate, but the Republican Party regained control of the House of Representatives, taking 83 seats from the Democrats. This was the biggest turnover in House seats since 1944 and demonstrated the widespread dissatisfaction with the state of the economy and the policies of the Obama administration. The Republican Party and the Tea Party movement were successful in winning control of the House because of the support of voters who were suffering – or were afraid they would suffer – from the consequences of the ongoing recession, such as unemployment, foreclosure on their homes and a further decline in their real incomes.

The result of this election was to deepen the legislative gridlock. The 112th US Congress, convened from January 2011 to January 2013, passed fewer laws than even the 80th Congress (1947–48), which President Harry Truman dubbed the "Do-Nothing Congress." Since January 2011 ideological partisan bickering over taxes and budgets has prevented legislative action, despite the serious financial and economic crises facing the country. The inability of the two parties to work together had the especially costly consequence of the House not raising the debt ceiling – a legislative limit on the amount of national debt that can be issued by the US Treasury – until the eleventh hour in both 2011 and 2013, thus bringing the US close to the brink of defaulting on its bonds.

Although the economy continued to struggle with a stubbornly high unemployment rate and a torpid growth rate, Obama was re-elected in November 2012, winning 51.1 percent of the total votes cast. The closeness of the votes won by Obama and Republican candidate Mitt Romney demonstrated how evenly and deeply the American electorate was divided. The Republican Party succeeded in retaining the House of Representatives, and legislative gridlock continued. Although the Republicans had to concede to an income tax increase for persons earning over $400,000, the two parties were unable to agree on fiscal and tax policies that could have reduced the national debt, then exceeding $14 trillion.

Because of the continuing legislative gridlock under this new Congress, reflecting the viscerally conflicting views of the parties and the voters, none of the major policies that had been debated for the past few years was resolved. These included reducing the national debt by achieving "a grand compromise," overhauling the complex and often unintelligible 72,536-pages-long tax law riddled with deductions and loopholes, and dealing with over 12 million immigrants living illegally in the US.

A stagnating economy and unemployment

The economy performed marginally better in 2013 than during the preceding few years, but it was still growing at a lackluster rate of below 2 percent. And, as was discussed in Chapter Four, the principal effect of the Federal Reserve Bank's continuing super-easy monetary policy was to increase asset prices and corporate profits without raising real wages or reducing unemployment. As a result, while total corporate profits as a proportion of GDP nearly doubled to 9.7 percent in 2012, up from 5 percent during the late 1980s, the same ratio for the total of wage and salary incomes declined from 52 percent during the 1980s to 42.6 percent in 2012. Even in 2013, the unemployment rate still hovered around 7.6 percent. Its decline from 8 percent in 2011 was due mostly to "the discouraged unemployed," who were no longer seeking employment and thus were not counted as unemployed. Furthermore, 58 percent of the jobs that were created during the 2010–12 period were low-paying jobs primarily in the service industries. These paid less than $14 per hour, or $28,000 per year, only $990 above the federal poverty level for a family of four in 2012.

An even more lamentable fact seen in the unemployment data from 2010 to 2014 is what was happening to the young. Although Americans of all ages suffered as a result of the Great Recession, the downturn dealt a particularly harsh blow to young people because most employers opted to hire from a suddenly plentiful pool of workers with more experience and a willingness to work at the prevailing low wage level. As a result, in 2014 nearly half of the unemployed were under 34 years old and many of the young people who were employed were overqualified for the jobs they were able to get. More than 40 percent of recent college graduates were working in jobs that did not require a degree.[7]

In late 2015, the "official" unemployment rate declined to 5 percent. However, the "official" unemployment rate is calculated as a ratio of those who are unemployed and actively seeking a job over the total labor force, which consists of everyone aged between 15 and 65 who is not in school. This ratio does not consider the discouraged unemployed, those unemployed who have given up looking for a job because their prior attempts have failed and they see no reason to try to find a job again. The number of such people increases when they see the growing number of people who are finding only very low-paying or part-time jobs. Since it is difficult to assess and measure people's motivations, the views on how to calculate the "real" unemployment rate by accounting for those who have given up seeking a job differ significantly among specialists concerned with measuring the unemployment rate. Many of them are convinced that the "real" unemployment rate is significantly higher than the official rate.[8]

One such person is James Clifton, CEO of the Gallup polling service, who wrote on February 14, 2015: "There's no other way to say this. The official unemployment rate, which cruelly overlooks the suffering of the long-term and often permanently unemployed as well as the depressingly underemployed, amounts to a Big Lie." And he went on to add that "the data released by the Bureau of Labor Statistics show hourly wages of all employees, measured at the 2015 price level, was 24.66 dollars in 2009 and 25.09 dollars in September of 2015. This is an increase of less than 2 percent in 6 years."[9]

Political paralysis

The stagnating economy was not the only critical issue faced by the second Obama administration. The political paralysis continued. From October 1 to 16, 2013, all but the critical parts of the US government were again shut down because the Republican-controlled House failed to enact legislation to appropriate funds for fiscal year 2014 if Obamacare was not defunded. The government re-opened only after some of the Republican House members relented and voted for the Appropriations Bill. This same Bill also raised the debt ceiling, thus enabling the Treasury Department to borrow more, once again averting the US government from defaulting on its debts.

That the Republicans were willing to shut down the government and threaten to force it to default on its debt indicates how far the they were willing to go to nullify Obamacare. The budget Bill that was passed was just an interim Bill that enabled Congress to "kick the can down the road", that is, to postpone for only a few months enacting a Bill to fund the 2015 budget. Furthermore, when the debt-ceiling crisis occurs again, the Treasury will be forced to ask for a higher ceiling, and the acrimonious debate and debt-default brinksmanship will be repeated. The continuing gridlock means that the US government has become a government that lurches from one crisis to the next.

It also has another very important consequence. The result of the 2014 mid-term election was that the Republican Party gained control of the Senate by 55 to 46 and increased its majority in the House to 247 Republicans vs. 188 Democrats. When Congress adjourned in December 2014, the total number of laws passed in the 2013–14 session was a mere 296, in comparison to 900 that were enacted by the "Do Nothing" Congress of 1947–48.

American politics has become not only gridlocked but also ideologically truculent. One of the few Bills that did make it through that lame-duck session of the House in December 2014 was the Bill funding the 2015 budget. (The session is called "lame duck" because it included those members who were defeated in the November election.) Attached to this Bill were two riders, de facto separate bills having little to do with the Bill to which they were attached, but which became law when the Bill was enacted.

One rider significantly weakened the Wall Street Reform and Consumer Protection Act enacted in 2010. The main goals of this ambitious Act, known as the Dodd-Frank Act, were to promote the financial stability of the US by improving accountability and transparency in the financial system; to end financial institutions being "too big to fail," in order to protect American taxpayers from being forced to bail out financial institutions in the future; and to protect consumers from abusive financial service practices. What the rider did was to effectively nullify a provision in the Dodd-Frank Act that prevented large banks from relying on the Federal Deposit Insurance Corp to bail them out if they faced a risk of bankruptcy by trading in risky assets. This rider was attached by a Republican Congressman who used almost verbatim a draft written by a lobbyist of Citigroup, one of the largest financial conglomerates in the US.[10]

The second rider effectively nullified the McCain-Feingold campaign finance law that was enacted in 2002. This law had limited individual contributions to a single committee of a political party to $32,400. The passage of the rider made it possible for an individual to contribute up to $1.6 million. This was in addition to what the Supreme Court had permitted in its decision in the *Citizens United v. Federal Trade Commission* case of 2010, which was to allow corporations and labor unions to donate unlimited funds during political campaigns to political committees advocating any political view. The Supreme Court's reasoning was that campaign contributions by corporations and unions cannot be limited because these donations are expressions of free will and thus protected by the First Amendment, guaranteeing the freedom of speech.

Conclusion

The American economy remains sluggish in 2016. Although the economic growth rate exceeded 2 percent in some quarters and stock prices and the profits of many firms are rising, the benefits are not trickling down to a large majority of the population. The respected Pew Research Institute, in its survey made in January 2015, found that 55 percent of Americans saw their real income "falling behind," while 37 percent found their real income "just keeping up with the rising cost of living." Median household real income was $53,013 in 2014, which was 7 percent below the pre-recession peak of $56,436 in 1999. Even near the end of 2015, almost 7 million fewer people were employed than when the Great Recession began in 2008. Moreover, some 40 percent of the newly created jobs in 2015 were lower-paying jobs in the service and other industries, and up to 15.8 percent of the young, aged between 18 and 29, were still underemployed in the early months of 2016.[11]

Put simply, the post-1980 economic stagnation continues, with all of its grave social and economic consequences, and there is no sign of the political gridlock abating, as is starkly evidenced in the 2016 campaigns by the candidates for the presidency. It is time for Americans to realize that they live in a new world and to make the necessary systemic change in their capitalism that will enable them to make much more investment to meet societal needs, which is the only way to reinvigorate their economy and democracy.

EIGHT

Japan: bubbles, "lost years" and Abenomics

Introduction

The Japanese economy entered its "bubble" years in the late 1980s, but the bubble burst in 1991, ushering in a period of economic stagnation that continues today. The economic policies adopted since 1991 have been pro-investment policies that are ineffective in the new world. The incompetent conservative and center-left governments of the 2009–12 period prolonged the stagnation, and since 2013 the government of the conservative Liberal Democratic Party has been pursuing a delusional variant of pro-investment policies. This chapter first discusses the bubble years and the period to 2008, and then the period from 2009 to the present.

The bubble and the "lost" years, 1980–2008

At the beginning of the 1980s, Japan was flying high. The economy was growing at almost 4 percent per year and many people in Japan and the West were touting Japanese economic institutions and practices as models the West should emulate. During the second half of the 1980s, the prices of stock and land both soared, the Japanese travelled abroad in unprecedented numbers and foreign investment by Japanese companies increased very rapidly. For example, Japanese FDI (foreign direct investment that does not include investments in stocks and bonds) in the US surged from $2 billion in 1985 to $20 billion in 1990.

The reason for the soaring prices of land and stocks during the second half of the 1980s was the Plaza Accord of 1985. This was an agreement among the US, Japan, West Germany, the UK and France to depreciate the dollar against the yen and the German mark. The request for the agreement came from the US, where industries were facing a significant competitive disadvantage because the value of the dollar had risen so strongly, especially against both the yen and the mark. Japan's central motivation in agreeing to the terms of the Accord was to minimize trade friction with the US, its most important customer. Also, the US was providing a "nuclear umbrella" under a bilateral mutual security treaty that enabled Japan to spend only 1 percent of its GDP on national defense, while Germany was spending about 3 percent and the US close to 6 percent of GDP on defense.

Immediately after the signing of the Plaza Accord, the Bank of Japan adopted a historic low interest rate policy in order to stimulate the economy lest it should falter due to the higher value of the yen, which it feared would reduce exports. The result of the lower interest rates was the "asset bubble" of the late 1980s, which was inevitable in the new world because the sudden increase in the supply of money was not needed for investment to increase productive capacity. Instead, the increased money supply encouraged the speculative buying of stocks and land.

As the Nikkei index (Japan's Dow-Jones index) rose from 9,900 to 11,600 yen during 1985 and soared to 38,915 by the end of December 1989, land prices reached astronomical heights. The value of land adjacent to the Imperial Palace in Tokyo was so high by 1990 that it led to estimates that the palace grounds – an area similar in size to Central Park in New York – were worth more than the entire real estate value of California![1]

Alarmed by the magnitude of the bubble, the Bank of Japan finally raised its interest rate late in December of 1990. But less than a month later, in January 1991, the bubble suddenly burst. The Nikkei stock index plummeted to 16,000 yen over the course of the year and the price of land also took a nose-dive. The result was a prolonged recession. At the same time, the anemic economy suffered from persistent deflation. At the end of the 1990s, many pundits were speaking of the "Lost Decade," and by 2005 the expression was changed to "The Lost Fifteen Years."

As the economy remained mired in a long stagnation, banks found themselves sitting on huge sums of non-performing loans, that is, debts that had little prospect of being repaid. Many banks went bankrupt. The government increased public expenditure, financing it by increasing the national debt. In 2001, the Bank of Japan resorted to a near-zero interest rate policy and for five years bought government bonds and other financial papers to increase the money supply. The latter is what came to be called QE after the Great Recession of 2007–08. But the total amount of QE was only about $110 billion (at the exchange rates of those years). The economy remained moribund.

In an effort to revitalize the economy, successive governments turned to public works projects. More roads, highways, bridges, airports and leisure facilities were built. These projects were chosen mainly to benefit the construction industry, a major supporter, both in cash and in votes, of successive conservative governments. The result of this public spending was to balloon the government deficit. The national debt-to-GDP ratio, which was already 75 percent in 1980, exceeded 174 percent by 2008, the highest among all the countries of the OECD.

Ineffective government

The party that was chiefly responsible for these developments was the Liberal Democratic Party (LDP), the largest conservative party, which was in power from 1980 to 2009 with the exception of the five years 1992–96. During those five years the country was governed by two unstable coalition governments, one led by the Japan Socialist Party (JSP) and the other consisting of several ideologically diverse conservative parties. In the election of 1996, the LDP regained power because of the ineffectiveness of the coalition governments and the crushing of the JSP (which went from 142 to 4 seats in the Lower House). The JSP lost support because, in order to lead a coalition government, it had compromised its long-held stance of rejecting the legitimacy of the Japan Self-Defense Forces and the US–Japan Security Treaty. (The JSP still believes that Article 9 of the Japanese constitution prohibited the country from having military forces, regardless what they were called.) The result of the 1996 election was to shift the center of gravity in Japanese politics further to the Right.

But the return of the LDP to power did not signify the return of an effective government. Between 1996 and 2009 there were seven LDP prime ministers. Five were lackluster and stayed in office only about a year. The two prime ministers worthy of note were Ryutaro Hashimoto and Jun'ichiro Koizumi. Hashimoto, who served as prime minister from 1996 to 1998, succeeded in opening Japanese markets to greater competition by easing foreign investment restrictions in sectors ranging from automobiles to insurance, banking and security exchanges. He also raised the consumption tax from 4 percent to 5 percent to help deal with the growing government deficit. But because the tax increase was seen as a major reason for the further erosion in the performance of the economy, the LDP had no choice but to replace Hashimoto.

Koizumi became prime minister in 2001 and remained in office until 2006, thus becoming the longest-serving Japanese prime minister since 1990. He was a maverick who succeeded in achieving some of his goals against the strong resistance of entrenched interest groups and a sizable faction within his own party. His most important successes were to slow the pace of the mounting government debt, to privatize the postal service (which also provided financial services in competition with private financial institutions) and to reform the banking system, which was still saddled with huge amounts of non-performing loans. Koizumi lasted as long as he did because the economy showed modest signs of growth and because many voters welcomed his maverick style.

Scandals involving graft and influence-peddling among LDP politicians plagued the LDP. Koizumi's successor, Shinzo Abe, lasted only one year in office. He resigned due to supposed ill health, as well as scandals in his cabinet. Each of the two uninspiring prime ministers who followed Abe also managed to stay in office for only about a year.

A stagnating economy

The economy continued to grow at less than 1.5 percent and even turned negative in a few quarters after 2006. Investments continued to stagnate and deflation became endemic. The main reason for the deflation was weakness of demand due to the new world of too much stuff. This was exacerbated by stagnating real wages, a rapidly aging population and a falling birthrate.

In the 1980s, Japan's per capita real income, measured by the internationally comparable purchasing power parity basis – the real purchasing power of a currency adjusted for exchange rate and determined for each country based on its relative cost of living and inflation rate – was the second-highest in the OECD economies. However, by 2008 it had declined to 19th. Japan's fiscal condition rapidly deteriorated even further as tax revenues continued to plummet while government expenditures increased. The total national debt to GDP rose to 194 percent in 2008. (For Greece, the same ratio in 2008 was 130 percent, and the average ratio for all eurozone economies was around 80 percent.)

By around 2005 the mass media and pundits had begun to discuss the possibility of Japan's becoming unable to sustain its finances because of its rapidly increasing national debt. This was mainly because the saving rate had declined from 16 percent during the 1980s to 2 percent by 2005, due to the slow-to-no increase in real wages and the aging of the population. The ability of the government to continue to sell 95 per cent of its bonds domestically while paying very low interest rates had to be questioned because the declining saving rate meant the decreasing ability of the Japanese to buy government bonds.

An important reason for economic stagnation was the declining international competitiveness of Japanese industries. In its annual report of 2009, the respected Swiss International Institute for Management Development ranked the competitiveness of Japanese industries 27th in the world, behind both China (18th) and South Korea (23rd). This decline in competitiveness was a major reason for stagnant real wages. Further weakening economic performance during these years was the accelerating decline in exports because of the rising value of the yen, which went from 130 yen to the dollar in 2001 to 90 yen to the dollar in 2008. The yen's steady appreciation was due to the sustained low interest rate policy of the Fed in the US, where the economy was suffering from the effects of the bursting of the dot.com bubble, followed by the Great Recession of 2007–08.

Changing employment practice

Another very significant development during the first decade of the new century was a steady crumbling of Japan's long-vaunted "permanent employment" system. After the bubble burst in 1991, the number of people hired on a non-permanent basis began to rise steadily. Non-permanent employees can be hired on a short-term or temporary basis, even when the employer intends them to work for the long term by repeatedly renewing their contracts. These employees are paid much lower wages and have few prospects of receiving the wage increases expected under the seniority-based, permanent employment system. They receive few benefits such as a paid vacation and maternity leave, although, like all Japanese, they are covered by national health insurance. In 1987 only 16 percent of the total labor force was employed on a temporary basis, but by 2009 that figure had doubled, to 32.8 percent. In addition, more and more large firms were reducing their numbers of permanent employees and instead using sub-contractors whose employees were paid substantially lower wages. This was one of the crucial reasons why the wages of an increasing number of earners stagnated or fell.

This trend in employment practices led to an increasing number of young people facing poverty. The proportion of unemployed among the young, defined as persons aged between 15 and 34, rose from around 4 percent in the 1980s to almost 9 percent by 2009. But unemployment was not the only problem that the younger generation faced. In 2008, among employees aged under 35, 23.1 percent of males and 46.5 percent of females were non-regular employees, in contrast to 9.1 percent of males and 23.2 percent of females in 1990. An increasing number of the young had become "freeters" (a Japanese word coined from "freelance" in English and "Arbeiter" in German), temporary or part-time employees who change jobs more often than do other non-regular employees. The Cabinet Office's *White Paper on Youth* estimated in 2009 that the number of freeters had risen from around 500,000 in 1982 to 1.7 million in 2008.

Furthermore, the number of persons aged between 15 and 34 who were "Not in Education, Employment or Training" (so-called NEETs) increased. According to the *Labor Force Survey*, between 1993 and 2009 the number of NEETs aged 15–29 increased from 400,000 to 640,000, while the number of NEETs aged 30–34 more than doubled, from 90,000 to 190,000. In evaluating the real significance of these numbers relating to freeters and NEETs, it is important to note that the total number of persons aged below 35 was decreasing during the 1980–2009 period because of the rapid aging of the Japanese population. This makes the rapid increase in numbers of freeters and NEETs even more significant.

Because policymakers have continued to adopt pro-investment policies that are ineffective in the new world, Japan's post-bubble economy has remained mired in chronic stagnation, persistent deflation, declining real wages, more people in insecure jobs and an increasing disparity in the distribution of income and wealth.

Government since 2009: from incompetent to delusional

In the Lower House election of 2009, the center-left Democratic Party of Japan (DPJ) trounced the LDP. The DPJ promised to move from a focus on "concrete" – all the tax-funded construction projects long favored by the LDP – to a focus on "people." Its number of seats in the Lower House soared from 113 to 308 out of a total of 480, while the LDP's number of seats plummeted, from 308 to 119. The strong performance of the DPJ was especially surprising, given that the party consisted of a rather motley group cobbled together from politicians from four ideologically diverse parties. Two of these parties included many defectors from the LDP, and the other two were mostly made up of former members of the Socialist Party, which had been all but decimated. For the LDP to lose in such a humiliating way to the recently created and ideologically ill-defined DPJ was one of the most monumental upsets in Japanese politics.

The chief reasons for the crushing defeat of the LDP were voters' mounting discontent over the still-lethargic economy, with the performance of the previous three successive LDP governments, each led by an uninspiring prime minister, and with a political party that was scandal-prone and inbred. In 2009, up to 35 percent of LDP members in both houses were the sons or other close relatives of former LDP politicians.

The DPJ's election "manifesto" promised to revitalize the economy by increasing expenditure on health, education and other programs. It also made a series of pledges that included reducing the corporate tax rate for small and medium-sized companies, strengthening the hi-tech and pro-environment industries, providing a child allowance and guaranteeing free high school education, and increasing expenditure on pensions and medical care.

What sounded good on paper, however, did not materialize in practice. The ideologically divided DPJ government failed to carry out many of the programs that it had promised because of its inability to fund them. The party also proved to be as unstable as the LDP had become, with three DPJ prime ministers in as many years.

We will never know whether history would have been kinder to the DPJ had the March 11, 2011 triple disaster not occurred in northeastern Japan: the devastating earthquake and tsunami and the nuclear reactor meltdowns at the Fukushima Daiichi nuclear power plant. What we do know, however, is that the party did not live up to the challenge of providing credible leadership at a time of national crisis. Moreover, like the LDP, the DPJ was pursuing a pro-investment policy based on supply-side economics.

Not surprisingly, the DPJ governments ended up significantly increasing the national debt because they "balanced" their budgets by covering almost half of the total expenditure through the sale of government bonds. In 2012, for example, 49 percent of the budget was "financed" by government bonds, which exceeded 7 percent of the GDP of that year. The economy failed to grow and wages continued to stagnate or slide. Although the unemployment rate was officially put at less than 4.5 percent, few Japanese economists dispute that the real rate was nearly 9 percent. This was disguised by a growing number of underemployed, freeters and NEETs, and also by generous government subsidies enabling firms to retrain or to retain redundant workers.

Data from the Ministry of Internal Affairs and Communications show that the proportion of non-permanent employees continued to increase, rising from 32.8 percent of the total number of employed in 2009 to 37.6 percent in 2013. The proportion of non-permanent employees was far higher for females than for males, at 52.9 percent compared to just 17.9 percent. And because the total numbers of NEETs and freeters remained at the high levels reached in 2009, and also because of the increase in the number of non-permanent employees, the total number of households living in "relative poverty" rose from 15.7 percent in 2009 to 17 percent by 2013. (Relative poverty is defined by the OECD as having a disposable income of less than half of the median household income.) Japan's percentage was the fourth-highest among the 34 OECD nations, following Mexico, Turkey and the US.

The DPJ's control of the government ended with the Lower House election of December 2012. The DJP, which had held 308 seats, now won only 57, while the LDP gained 294 seats, more than doubling the 119 it had held before the election. The LDP now had a comfortable majority in the Lower House even without relying on the 31 seats that the CGP, the Clean Government Party, held after the election.

The CGP is a Buddhist party that has been in coalition with the LDP since 1998.

"Abenomics"

With the LDP win, Shinzo Abe became prime minister for a second time. He quickly appointed Haruhiko Kuroda as the new governor of the Bank of Japan. Kuroda strongly supported Abe's vision of "an unprecedentedly bold monetary policy" to increase the supply of money in order to end the continuing deflation and revitalize the economy. In January 2013 the Bank of Japan and the government signed an accord with two main terms. First, the Bank was to sharply increase the monetary base (the total amount of currency circulating in the hands of the public and held in easily accessible demand deposits) at a rate exceeding the rates that had been maintained by all other major central banks since 2008. This was in order to reach the goal of 2 per cent inflation within two years. Second, the government was to do its best to re-establish Japan's fiscal credibility, that is, to reduce the debt to GDP ratio, which had reached 240 percent of GDP, the highest in the world.[2]

Based on this accord, the Abe government announced the details of an ambitious economic policy that was quickly dubbed "Abenomics." The policy consisted of what Abe termed the "three arrows."

1. Public spending of 13 trillion yen (about $118 billion at 110 yen to a dollar or 2.5 percent of GDP) would be made during the 2013–14 fiscal year. In addition, the government planned to spend up to 200 trillion yen during the next decade in order to stimulate the economy. The increased government expenditure would be financed by tax revenues, which were expected to increase because of an assumed annual real GDP growth rate of at least 2 percent.
2. To reach the inflation target of 2 percent, the Bank of Japan would double the monetary base within two years by adding an amount equivalent to 1 percent of GDP, or $60 billion, every month. This rate of increase is twice what the US Federal Reserve Bank maintained between 2008 and 2013

when adjusted for the difference in size of the two countries' GDPs. To achieve this goal, the Bank of Japan would buy Japanese government bonds of a longer maturity, that is, of up to five years, which the Bank had hitherto declined to do.

3. Structural reforms would be carried out over an unspecified number of years in order to assure that the real GDP would increase by an average real rate of 2 percent per year over the next decade. The proposed reforms consisted of many vaguely stated, ambitious plans that were certain to meet very strong opposition from numerous entrenched and powerful interest groups. Most significant among the very long list was the passage of laws to help increase investment and liberalize the labor market, and measures to enable more women to work, to promote innovation, upgrade infrastructure, use land more efficiently, make agriculture more competitive internationally and create free trade zones as part of liberalizing international trade.

Since Abenomics is an extremely bold macroeconomic policy experiment based on supply-side economics, and the ineffectiveness and consequences of supply-side economics have already been discussed in the preceding chapters, we will now turn to examine the outcomes of Abe's policies.

The outcomes of Abenomics

Since 2013, when Abe's policies were put in place, the average quarterly real growth rate of the economy has been only 0.6 percent. Despite an almost 20 percent depreciation of the yen, the quarterly trade balance has frequently turned negative because the prices of imports have risen, due to the depreciation of the yen. The real wages of a large majority of employees have remained stagnant or are sliding and the disparity in the distribution of income and wealth has increased. As of April 2016, none of the "third arrow" plans that could have claimed positive results has been carried out because the government has not been able to overcome the entrenched power of interest groups.

There were initial signs of the possible success of Abenomics. The Nikkei index rose almost 60 percent during the spring of 2013, principally because of the rapidly increasing monetary base. The mass media reported the news of increasing exports of automobiles, electronics and a few other products, and so the LDP won a resounding victory in the Upper House election in the summer of 2013. The LDP itself won 115 seats and its ally, the CGP, won 20. Before the election, the 242-seat Upper House was controlled by opposition parties, with the LDP holding only 84 seats and the CGP a mere 19, but this victory gave the LDP control of both houses in the Diet.

Spurred on by early evidence of the seeming success of Abenomics and by its victory in the Upper House election, the government continued to implement the first two arrows of Abenomics, the Bank of Japan continued to expand the monetary base as promised and the government proceeded to implement its expansionary fiscal policy.

However, during 2013 and 2014 the living standard of a large majority of Japanese continued to deteriorate. While wages remained stagnant, the cost of imported necessities (food and energy) continued to rise because of the depreciated yen. And in April 2014 the government raised the regressive sales tax from 5 to 8 percent.

In October of 2014, the Bank of Japan surprised the markets by announcing that it would increase QE by augmenting the purchase of government bonds from an amount equivalent to $60 billion per month to $80 billion per month. Then, on November 21, the prime minister suddenly dissolved the Lower House and called a snap election, to be held on December 21. (In the Japanese parliamentary system the prime minister can call an election before the end of the legally determined term of the parliament, and he will do so if he believes it to be politically advantageous. In this case, the election was called two years in advance of the legally required date.) Abe had several reasons for his decision to call an election. First, he wanted to reaffirm his electoral mandate in order to continue Abenomics. But second, he also wanted to proceed with his nationalistic policies to enable Japan to participate in "collective defense," that is, to use Japan's military forces for more than just self-defense, and to increase the defense budget and export more weapons. He also wanted to strengthen his position in the LDP and retain the party leadership, and he wanted to further weaken the DPJ and other parties, which were unprepared for an election.

The results of the election were as Abe had hoped. He had campaigned with the slogan "There is no alternative to Abenomics." As Abe himself admitted, he had emulated the slogan of "TINA" – "There Is No Alternative" – used by Margaret Thatcher in England during the 1980s.[3] Even though the LDP lost two seats, its coalition partner, the CGP, gained four, giving the coalition a net gain of two seats. The coalition now held 326 seats out of the total 475.

Two years into Abenomics, some of the results had become unmistakable. The first two "arrows" were creating a minority of "winners" and a majority of "losers." The winners were mainly holders of assets, especially stocks, who benefited from the rising price of their stocks. They also included the shareholders, officers and employees of the largest firms in the automobile and several other industries whose exports were increasing.

The losers were people who held few or no assets, plus approximately 70 percent of employees, most of whom were working in small and medium-sized firms in non-exporting and service industries. According to data released by the Ministry of Welfare and Labor in April 2015, the total monthly cash income received by all workers in February 2015 was only 0.5 percent higher than that in February 2014. This means that, because of the increase in prices due to the 3 percent increase in the consumption tax, the real wage level had declined. The real wage level reached its peak in 1997 and has stagnated ever since. In 2015, it was down by 13.9 percent from the 1997 level. And the 2015 data provided by the Ministry of Welfare and Labor show that the proportion of non-permanent employees exceeded 40 percent of the total labor force. In short, Abenomics has not had the trickle-down effect of creating a virtuous cycle of increased asset prices and exports, leading to increased real wages and demand.

Japan's budget for 2015 was $814 billion, converted at the prevailing exchange rate of 120 yen to the dollar. It was "balanced" by the sale of government bonds, as have been all of the budgets since 1990. To balance the 2015 budget, $356 billion worth of government bonds, amounting to 43.7 percent of the total budget, had to be sold. This is an amount approximately equivalent to 7.3 percent of GDP, the highest budget deficit to GDP ratio in 2015 among the OECD economies. The main reasons for such a budget were the steadily increasing spending on social welfare (mostly for medical and nursing care for the elderly) and the high cost of servicing the debt (about $200 billion, or approximately 24 percent of the total budget).

There is little prospect of the Abe administration's being able to achieve the goal of structural reform described in "the third arrow." This is because Abe will be unable to keep his promise of "drilling against the expected bedrock of the likely strong opposition of interest groups to make substantive structural changes that will increase the performance of the economy."[4] The LDP government is reliant on "the bedrock" for votes and campaign contributions, and so the Abe administration is not at all likely to make a serious attempt to "drill the bedrock" in order to succeed in making the promised structural reforms.

Other policies

The Abe administration, while extremely loquacious about most of its policies, has been very reticent in discussing its environmental policy. Abe himself has said little. And the chief Japanese delegate at the UN climate change conference in Lima, Peru in December 2014 was harshly criticized for Japan's inability to support the draft resolution asking each of nearly 200 nations to specify their respective goals for the reduction of carbon emissions.[5]

The Abe administration has continued Japan's unusually restrictive immigration policy. During the decade since 2005, Japan granted citizenship to no more than between 9,000 and 15,000 immigrants per year. These figures are far lower than those of all the other developed economies. Barring a totally unlikely sudden increase in the birthrate, Japan's total population, which was 126.5 million in 2015, will decline to between 90 and 100 million by 2060. This means that total demand will continue to decline, the labor shortage will become acute and it will become impossible for the government to pay the increasing costs of caring for the aged, whose proportion in the total population is increasing faster than in any other developed economy. The country cannot but become less innovative and productive. But the Abe administration is only now discussing a policy that would permit recruiting from abroad an unspecified annual number of "highly skilled" workers and "nurses and others who assist the aged."

Meanwhile, a decline in the voter participation rate in elections reflects a "hollowing of democracy" that is replicated in other developed countries. In the April 2015 elections for governors in 10 prefectures and the members of 41 prefectural assemblies, the turnout was the lowest ever. The average turnout for the gubernatorial elections was 47.14 percent, and for the prefectural assemblies it was 45.05 percent.[6]

Conclusion

Abe's delusion continues. Despite the failure of the policies in the "three arrows" of 2013, he announced "three new arrows" on September 24, 2015. These new arrows consist of increasing Japan's GDP by 20 percent within an unspecified number of years, providing assistance for childrearing and strengthening safety nets. The first arrow is preparatory to justifying a proposal within the administration to reduce the tax rate on corporations to 20 percent as soon as possible. The second is to increase the birthrate so that Japan's population will be at least 100 million by mid-century. It is also intended to increase the labor participation rate of women so as to cope with the looming labor shortage. And the third arrow is to bolster the country's welfare services to create a society where no one needs to leave their job in order to care for elderly parents.

The three new arrows are an expression of unrealistic goals. In the new world in which the economy is so often in recession, as it was in 2015, the idea of achieving 20 percent growth in GDP in the near future is fanciful. Without a drastic change in the immigration policy, to think that Japan could have a population of 100 million people by mid-century is totally quixotic because the birthrate is continuing to decline and is unlikely to rise in the near future. And the quality of the safety nets will not be upgraded because Japan, with the world's highest debt-to-GDP ratio, is struggling even to maintain its current frayed safety nets.

There is no need to add further observations and data as of spring 2016 to show that the delusional Abenomics will continue to fail, because on April 11 the IMF downgraded its forecast for Japan's economic growth rate in 2016 from 1 percent to 0.5 percent. Its forecast for 2017 is *minus* 0.1 percent. What Japan needs is not these delusional old and new "arrows" but for its citizens to recognize that they are living in a new world and to make a systemic change in their capitalism.

NINE

Unified Germany: a divided nation

Introduction

Germany has a long tradition of "soziale Marktwirtschaft" or "social market economy" that began during the 19th century and evolved into the post-Second World War West German capitalist economic system. This was a system that aspired to maintain "social equity" by endeavoring to have adequate social welfare, labor unions participation in management and other institutions and practices that would balance the power of capital and labor. However, after West Germany entered the new world during the 1980s and West Germany and East Germany were unified in 1990, German politics shifted to the Right and the government began to adopt pro-investment policies. Since then, Germany has suffered from economic stagnation and increasing disparities in the distribution of income and wealth. This chapter first highlights the developments of the period 1980–2008 and then examines the years since 2009, during which pro-investment policies and fiscal austerity became entrenched at the cost of trampling on the tradition of a social market economy.

1980–2008: German politics move to the Right

By the 1980s, the West German economy was no longer a postwar "Wirtschaftswunder" or economic miracle. During the 1990s, West Germany's exports were still doing moderately well, with an average trade surplus of around 2 per cent of GDP. But GDP was growing distinctly more slowly than it had done during the immediate postwar decades. The average growth rate was less than 2 percent and the unemployment rate hovered between 7 and 8 percent.

From 1982 to 1998, Helmut Kohl, of the center-right Christian Democratic Union (CDU), served as chancellor.[1] Kohl played the leading role both in the unification of Germany and in establishing the European Union. He did away with numerous government regulations and privatized Volkswagen, Lufthansa and many other large, state-owned enterprises. After unification in 1990, he was forced to raise taxes in order to help the former East Germany, but he was a fiscal conservative who always tried to minimize taxes.

The consequences of unification

Unification inflicted massive problems on the country. The centrally planned, inefficient economy of the East had to be reshaped and employment had to be found for the East German workers, who increased Germany's total labor force by almost one third. However, finding jobs for a large number of unemployed East Germans was extremely difficult because many were inadequately trained for immediate employment in an open, competitive market economy. And the effort to raise the East German wage level to the comparatively high West German level as quickly as possible posed formidable difficulties.

During the 1990s, the former East Germany continued to experience rising unemployment. It depended on federal subsidies and various other transfer payments paid for by the "solidarity tax" imposed on West Germans. These payments reached an equivalent of over $2 trillion before the end of the century. The economic growth rate for the country as a whole averaged less than 2 percent during the 1990s, while the unemployment rate was about 9 percent in the West and over 18 percent in the East. By the beginning of the new century, when the US, the UK, France and most other developed economies were performing better, Germany was called "the sick man of Europe."

Gerhard Schroeder and Agenda 2010

Because of the problems Germany faced, the CDU lost power in 1998. Gerhard Schroeder, of the Social Democratic Party (SPD), became chancellor and served for two terms (1998–2005). Upon taking office he adopted a wide-ranging policy that included funding for research and the adoption of renewable energies, recognition of same-sex marriage and liberalizing the naturalization laws. In his second term he pursued what he called "Agenda 2010," which was distinctively to the Right of traditional SPD policy. The centerpiece of Agenda 2010 was the Hartz reform (named after Peter Hartz, chairman of the commission that drafted the reform), which was carried out between 2003 and 2005. Its goals were to change the welfare system and to free the labor market from numerous regulations and entrenched practices that restricted employment practice.

Although the complex Hartz reform was aimed at "liberalizing" employment practices and reducing welfare spending, in particular unemployment benefits and social assistance, it also lowered tax rates for high-income earners. The reform benefited manufacturing industries because they could now employ temporary workers, who were hired from temporary employment agencies and paid much lower wages than regular employees. The biggest beneficiary of the reform was the automobile industry, which, although it faced strong opposition from labor unions, was able to reduce its wage bills and flexibly adjust it workforce to changing market conditions. The reform also reduced the employment protection of employees in the public sector and various other segments of the labor market. In addition, it severely curtailed funding for the Active Labor Market Policy, which focused on training and job creation paid for through public funds.

Agenda 2010, with the Hartz reform at its core, increased the unemployment rate from 10.5 percent in 2003 to 11.7 percent in 2005. The reform virtually froze the real wage level of most employees and forced those employed in the "mini-jobs" created by the reform to live on financially insecure low incomes. These mini-jobs were (and still are) part-time jobs created by employers to take advantage of the reform's elimination of payroll tax on employees earning less than €400 per month (raised to €450 in 2011). Because the economy grew by only 1.2 percent in 2004 and 0.7 percent in 2005, and also because of the high unemployment rate and all the other consequences of the reform, including widening disparity in both wage and income distribution, the SPD lost control of the government in the election of 2005.

Angela Merkel and the recovery of the sick man of Europe

The new government formed in 2005 was a grand coalition of the CDU and the SPD, since neither party had a majority in the Bundestag (the lower house). In the end, Angela Merkel won a protracted negotiation with the SPD and became the first female chancellor in German history. But under the terms of the grand coalition she was hamstrung in implementing policy and had to give 8 of 16 cabinet posts to the SPD, one of which was the critical post of minister of finance. Despite these limitations, Merkel pursued a conservative small government policy of reducing the budget deficit and eliminating a wide variety of government regulations. But she also adopted policies to mitigate the decline in the birthrate, such as providing working parents with more funding for childcare.

During the first three years of Merkel's five-year term the economy began to grow because of increasing exports both within the EU and to China and other emerging economies. An important reason why Germany was able to increase its exports within the EU was the adoption of the euro in 1999, which helped the eurozone economies to increase their economic growth rates, thus enabling them to import more from Germany. The higher growth rate was a result of (1) the increased ability of eurozone countries to borrow money on the international capital markets at low real interest rates and (2) the gains realized due to elimination of the risk and transaction costs involved in using multiple currencies. The increased German exports to emerging economies arose from steadily growing demand for high-quality machinery, automobiles and chemical products, most of which were produced by Germany's celebrated small and medium-sized firms, called "Mittelstand."

The growth rate of German GDP rose to 2.8 percent in 2006 and 3.4 percent in 2007, while the unemployment rate, which was at 11 percent in 2005, fell gradually to 8 percent by 2008. Germany's trade surplus steadily rose from 2 percent of GDP to the 5–6 percent range during 2007 and 2008. The budget improved rapidly, from a deficit that was the equivalent of 4 percent of GDP in 2005 to a balanced budget in both 2007 and 2008. Because the economy was beginning to grow, Merkel's approval rating remained high – at 80–85 percent during 2007 and into 2008 – and many in the mass media began to say that "the sick man of Europe" had recovered.

Rising inequality

However, the improved economic performance of these years was achieved at the cost of visibly increasing the disparity in distribution of income and wealth. Due first to the policy of liberalizing the labor market under the Schroeder administration, and then because of the pro-business tax and subsidy policies of Merkel's government, labor's share (wages and salaries) of GDP declined vis-à-vis capital's share (profits and rents). The Federal Statistical Office in Wiesbaden reported that while labor's share of GDP fell from 71.2 percent in 2005 to 67.2 percent in 2008, capital's share rose from 28.8 percent to 32.8 percent during the same period. And, as was noted in Chapter Five, the Gini coefficient (after taxes and transfers) rose from 0.265 in 2000 to 0.285 in 2005, and then to 0.295 in 2008. This meant that the coefficient, which had been close to the low Scandinavian level in 2000, had crept up to close to the OECD average of 0.300 by 2008.

Observing these developments, an October 2008 OECD study, *Increasing Social Inequality and Poverty in Germany*, noted:

> For a long period following the war, income disparity in Germany remained relatively small compared to other countries. Now Germany has nearly reached the OECD average ... The number of households without any earned income has increased from 15.2 to 19.4 percent. Currently nearly one fifth of households are dependent on some sort of state benefit, the highest level of all OECD countries.

Germany, like Japan and several European countries, is seeing clear trends of a decreasing birthrate and the aging of the population. But, unlike Japan, Germany has a high rate of immigration, which is preventing the overall population from shrinking. Even so, the ratio of working people to elderly pensioners has been decreasing. By 2008, the ratio was only 2.2. Estimates based on demographic trends indicate that within the next decade the ratio will be less than 2, meaning that fewer than two workers must support one pensioner. This development is the reason why the coalition government has adopted various policies designed to increase the birthrate, such as raising child benefit and increasing the number of kindergartens.

The Great Recession

Because of Germany's sustained trade surpluses, its financial institutions were making huge loans and global investments. This meant that the country was adversely affected by the Great Recession that began in 2007. During 2008, the government had to abandon its hope of balancing the budget because tax revenues were declining rapidly. GDP contracted by 5.1 percent and a fiscal stimulus of €50 billion had to be made by the end of the year.

In 2008, German exports, the engine of the country's economic growth, had declined by 7.1 percent to countries within the EU and by 1.6 percent to countries outside the EU.

And in October 2008, with the imminent bankruptcy of Hypo Real Estate Holding AG, a holding company of several large real estate financing banks with total assets of almost €200 billion, the government had to adopt a rescue package of €35 billion. The government also enacted a financial market stabilization law in order to establish a fund of up to €400 billion to be used to help assure the stability of German financial institutions.

At the end of 2008, few Germans could have predicted the roles that their government and the country's financial resources would have to play in the extremely serious crises of the euro and the financial institutions of the EU that would continue in the coming years.

From 2009 to the present: the high cost of Merkel's policies

Recovery from the financial crisis

The German economy recovered from the immediate very serious effects of the global financial crisis faster than did other economies of the EU, albeit from the suddenly shrunken base of GDP in 2008. The economic growth rate rebounded to 4.2 percent by 2010 and 3.0 percent in 2011. And although the unemployment rate increased in 2009, it was by less than 0.5 percent, and returned to the pre-crisis level of 7 percent in 2010 and 2011. The trade surplus fell from $178 billion in 2008 to $139 billion in 2009, but quickly rebounded, to $220 billion in 2010 and $215 billion in 2011.

Despite a decline in global trade during these years, German exports continued to recover, for two main reasons: (1) the international competitiveness of its industrial firms, which is due to their well-established technological strengths, and (2) since 2003, a significantly lower increase in real wage rates than in other OECD countries, especially those of the EU, the most important importers of German products. Data show that labor productivity in German manufacturing industries rose faster than the real wage level from 2005 to 2013 (the last year for which reliable labor productivity data are available). It is important to understand that the fact that real wages were rising less than labor productivity was the main reason for Germany's export prowess. But the inevitable negative result was capital's increasing share of GDP, that is, a widening disparity in income distribution.

Mainly because of the fiscal stimulus and expenditure to help financial institutions, the budget deficit increased sharply, by 3.1 percent of GDP in 2009 and 4.1 percent 2010, levels that breached the 3 percent limit agreed upon by euro-using members of the EU. However, because of increasing tax revenue provided by the slow but steady growth of GDP and the Merkel government's pursuit of fiscal austerity, the budget was nearly balanced in 2011 (the deficit amounted to only 0.8 percent of GDP) and there was a small surplus (0.2 percent) in 2012.

Since 2009, as several economies of the eurozone have faced budgetary and banking crises and even the future of the euro has begun to be questioned, Germany has become what *The Economist* has aptly called "The Reluctant Hegemon." Germany was forced to provide political and financial leadership in order to save the euro and help solve the budgetary and banking crises of several members of the eurozone. Merkel has had the unenviable task of balancing her desire to save the euro and several eurozone members from their financial crises against her desire not to increase the burden on German taxpayers, both for the sake of retaining her political base and to avoid deviating from her own conservative principles. As stated by Jürgen Habermas, a leading German sociologist and philosopher, her task has been that of "the leader of the German government which holds the key to the fate of the European Union in its hands. The main question is whether Germany is not only in a position to take the initiative, but also whether it could have an interest in doing so."[2]

Because of Merkel's popularity, which reflected the strength of the conservative narrative based on supply-side economics and the voters' reluctance to change their chancellor in the midst of an economic crisis, the CDU/CSU won an easy victory in the election held in September 2009. With the help of its ally, the small center-right FDP (Free Democratic Party), Merkel won a second five-year term as chancellor. Now she could exercise power without the constraints imposed by the SPD, as had been the case in the grand coalition government. In numerous polls throughout 2010 and 2011, Merkel's popularity ranged between 62 and 74 percent, indicating the voters' high confidence in her, while the popularity of her party, the CDU, was much lower, fluctuating between 38 and 40 percent.

"Energiewende"

In May 2011, only two months after the huge earthquake and tsunami caused a devastating nuclear accident in Fukushima, Japan, Merkel announced that her government would immediately close down 8 of 17 operating nuclear reactors and would close the remaining ones by 2022. This was a sudden and drastic change in energy policy, dubbed the "Energiewende" (energy turn), because nuclear plants provided 17.7 percent of the national electricity supply. But Merkel was willing to face the political costs of adopting this policy, which would raise the cost of electricity to consumers and impose high costs on the nuclear energy industry. She was convinced that "Energiewende" would enable Germany both to move towards the use of renewable energies and to create jobs and develop and export new technologies.

Merkel's views on energy and the environment were in sharp contrast to those of Japanese Prime Minister Abe, who supported restarting the operation of Japan's nuclear energy plants, which had all been shut down following the nuclear disaster in Fukushima, as quickly as possible. As noted in the preceding chapter, Abe has had little to say on environmental policies.

Voter discontent

Critics of the Merkel government's domestic policies grew increasingly vocal as 2012 wore on. They were unhappy with the underfunding of social welfare programs, as well as with the chancellor's new energy policy, which was increasing the price of energy. Voters criticized her reluctance to support a national minimum wage law, to make larger increases in both childcare subsidies and allowances for parents who were caring for small children at home and to increase funding to support public transportation.

As a result of the smoldering criticism and voters' increasing perception that Merkel was too focused on fiscal austerity and too accommodating of the EU policy of aiding the eurozone economies in financial crisis at the expense of German taxpayers, her party was badly defeated in the March 2012 state in North Rhine-Westphalia, a rich, industrialized state with a population of nearly 18 million.

However, from 2012 and into the summer of 2013, while other eurozone economies were again in a recession and the economic growth rate of China and other emerging countries was decelerating, the German economy managed to avoid a recession for the same two reasons as it had done ever since 2003: its export industries were internationally competitive and real wages remained suppressed.

Further rising inequality

Although the German economy has managed to avoid a recession, the country has seen increasing inequality in the distribution of income and wealth, due mainly to the rightward shift in its economic policy since 2003. Chapter Five provided some data on this, but here we present more. In the spring of 2013, 14 percent of Germans were living in poverty, defined as persons earning less than 60 percent of the median income. At the same time, the number of millionaires (in dollar terms) stood at around 430,000, the highest number ever. This number had grown steadily since the beginning of the century, and rose rapidly, by 23 percent, between 2000 and 2013.

A report issued in 2015 by DIW (Deutsche Institut für Wirtschaftsforschung), the leading economic research institute in Berlin, reinforced these facts:

> These trends of an increasing disparity of income and wealth distribution have serious implications for the health of the society as a whole because the rising

wealth of the country has not led to prosperity for all, the great rallying cry of postwar Germany.[3]

In a survey by the magazine *Stern* that was published in February 2013, 58 percent of respondents said that "Income inequality and more broadly, social justice, is at the top of the political agenda." *Stern* commented, "We are certain to see income disparity become the main issue in the campaign for federal elections in the autumn."

In the election of September 2013, the CDU received only 42 percent of the vote and failed to obtain a majority in the Bundestag. Angela Merkel was unable to form a new CDU-led government with the party's current coalition partner, the FDP, which lost all of its members in the Bundestag. (The party failed to garner the minimum necessary 5 percent of the total votes to elect a member.) As a result, Merkel was forced once again to form a grand coalition government with the SPD, which was pledging to redress the increased disparity in the distribution of income and wealth.

At the urging of the SPD, Germany's first minimum wage law was enacted in July 2014. This law set the minimum wage at €8.50 (about $11.50), to start in 2015. Labor unions fiercely objected to its delayed promulgation and to the exemption of several categories of jobs. Even though the minimum wage is significantly higher than in the US,[4] the SPD and labor unions continue to argue that the law must be considered as only a first step if Germany is to rectify stagnant real wages, the principal reason for the increasing disparity in income distribution.

It is apparent that in enabling Merkel to remain chancellor, a sufficient number of voters had decided to support the CDU's pro-investment fiscal policies and Merkel's ideological belief in small government, at the cost of continuing disparity in income distribution. By staying the course with Merkel, German voters were also rejecting the increasing criticism of other EU members who were arguing that the export-led German economy was adopting a beggar-thy-neighbor policy. That is, German domestic demand was only increasing slowly because real wages were being suppressed and a low increase in domestic demand was limiting German imports from other EU economies, thus enabling Germany to have by far the largest trade surplus per capita among the large developed economies.

Further challenges at home

In recent years, a growing number of Germans have became anti-euro and anti-immigration, as in all other EU nations. Thus, Germany now has a new populist right-wing, anti-euro, anti-immigration party, which was formed in 2013. This is the Alternative for Germany Party – Alternative für Deutschland or AfD. The AfD won 7 out of 98 German seats in the 2014 elections for the European Parliament and has also won a significant number of votes in recent elections for state assembly members (around 10 percent of votes in 2014 in Saxony, Brandenburg and Thuringia, all in the former East Germany, and 7.4 percent in February 2015 in Hamburg, in the former West Germany). Although it is unlikely that the party will be a serious contender in national elections, the emergence and strength of the AfD and the declining rate of voter participation in elections are clear signs that democracy in Germany is now facing an increasing challenge, just as it is in all other developed economies.

In 2015 Germany faced an additional challenge, one that is likely to have many lingering effects into the future: massive immigration both by asylum seekers from war-torn countries in the Middle East and Afghanistan and by desperate economic migrants from numerous countries, amounting to well over 1 million in 2015. This immigration has continued in 2016, even though the numbers have dwindled in comparison to the pace in 2015. Although Germany can benefit from the addition to its labor force in the future, the task of providing for the welfare of so many and integrating them into German society will likely be very difficult.

Conclusion

However, the principal problem facing Germany today is its small government based on supply-side economics, which means that it is focused on fiscal austerity at the cost of widening disparity in the distribution of income and wealth. This fact is aptly summarized an article entitled "Germany Can Take that Smug Look Off Its Face," published on April 8, 2016 by Lucian Kim.[5]

> If a *Der Spiegel* cover is any indication of the mood in Germany, then Europe's largest country is on the verge of an explosion. Two weeks ago, the newsmagazine highlighted the country's growing income inequality in a cover story on "the divided nation." The cover photo showed a couple in a gilded room with a dozen other people stooped in a claustrophobic cellar below them … The headline screamed "You guys up there are just lying to us all" over a paint-spattered image of German Chancellor Angela Merkel.
>
> A yawning wealth gap and a voter rebellion nobody wanted to admit existed aren't unique to the United States. Across the industrialized world, the middle class is finding it increasingly difficult to make ends meet, while the losers of globalization are channeling their aggression into fringe politicians who know who's to blame. Modern Germany, a paragon of social peace and political moderation, is no exception.

Staying with the Merkel-led pro-investment fiscal policy and small government has exacerbated inequality in the distribution of income and wealth. It means that the government has neglected to make the socially necessary investments that are essential to enable capitalism in Germany to survive and thrive into the future. Germans have a long tradition of a "social market." Now they must become the leaders in recognizing that they are now living in a new world and that their capitalism must be systemically changed.[6]

TEN

Four European
economies

Introduction

The three largest developed economies are not the only countries whose capitalism is in a systemic crisis. Since it is not possible to discuss every developed capitalist democracy, this chapter presents a very brief summary of the economic performance, political developments and economic policies adopted in France, the UK, Italy and Spain since the 1980s. The four economies represent almost a score of other rich, democratic economies that include other countries in Europe and in the rest of the world, such as Canada, South Korea, Australia and New Zealand.

The four countries reviewed here have all seen their economies grow only slowly since the 1980s because they have adopted various pro-investment policies, at the cost of increasing disparities in income and wealth and failing to invest to meet their societies' needs. They too are facing a systemic crisis of capitalism that is threatening their democracies, and all for the same reason: their pro-investment economic policies are ineffective in the new world of too much stuff. As in the three preceding chapters, this survey looks first at the period 1980–2008 and then at the period from 2009.

From the 1980s to 2008

France

We begin with France, the economy second to Germany in GDP among the EU nations. France is an example of a country where neither socialist nor conservative governments were able to help the country's economy to grow by even 3 percent per year during this period.

The economic policies of Socialist President François Mitterrand (1981–95) included the nationalization of a dozen of the largest industrial firms and banks, but his policies failed to reduce the high rates of both unemployment and inflation. The economic growth rate averaged just 0.5 percent between 1981 and 1985. Economic conditions improved between 1986 and 1994, but the average growth rate for these years was still only 2.12 percent. From 1995 to 2007, Jacques Chirac, of the conservative party UMP (L'Union pour un Mouvement Populaire), served as president. His administration privatized Renault and a few dozen other large, nationally owned enterprises and reduced regulations on business and financial institutions in an effort to spur the growth rate. However, the average growth rate during his presidency fell to only 1.08 percent.

During the Chirac administration, the unemployment rate remained high, ranging between 10 and 12 percent. The trade balance deteriorated because French industry was lagging behind in the adoption of new technology and was burdened by inflexible labor market practices, and thus was becoming less competitive internationally. Also, the government still owned more large, inefficient businesses than was the case in most other EU economies, and this played a critical role in suppressing economic growth. Equally critical was Chirac's reduction of the budget deficit, especially during his first term, in order to meet the euro-using EU members' requirement of a maximum deficit of 3 percent of GDP. When the global financial crisis occurred in 2008, France's GDP contracted sharply, by 3.15 percent.

The UK

In the United Kingdom, the Conservative government led by Margaret Thatcher (1979–90) aggressively pursued many small government policies that included reducing expenditure on safety nets and privatizing state-owned enterprises, as well as adopting a pro-investment fiscal policy. These policies all proved to be unsuccessful. The economic growth rate during the 1980s averaged just 2.13 percent. Thatcher's policies of closing government-owned enterprises and reducing the budget deficit doubled unemployment in just three years, from 1.5 million in 1979 to over 3 million by 1982. Unemployment rose to 3.3 million in 1984, before beginning to decline very slowly to 1.6 million in 1990.

By any objective standard, it is indisputable that "Thatcherism," based on supply-side economics, was a failure. Thatcher's pro-investment fiscal policy, which included reducing the tax rate on the incomes of the wealthiest from 83 percent to 60 percent, was ineffectual in the new world, since the country had excess productive capacity in most industries. Demand did not increase for several reasons. VAT (sales tax) was raised from 8 percent to 15 percent, demand for necessary luxuries grew only slowly and real wages remained stagnant, due in large part to the laws Thatcher's administration adopted to restrict labor union activities. Disparity in income distribution grew because of her pro-investment fiscal policy and the reduced regulation of the activities of financial institutions, which favored the wealthy either directly or indirectly. While the financial sector prospered, the manufacturing sector continued to lose its international competitiveness because it fell behind other large industrialized economies in investment, technological change, R&D expenditure and for other reasons, thus becoming an important factor in the UK's chronic trade deficit.

The British economy suffered a serious recession in 1992, during Conservative Party John Major's prime ministership (1990–97). This recession kept the average growth rate for the period at only 0. 68 percent and the average unemployment rate at 7.8 percent, while real wages stagnated. Thus, in 1997, voters returned the Labour Party to power, led by Tony Blair. During

Blair's 10 years in office the economy grew at an average rate of 2.4 percent. Although his government enacted the first national minimum wage law in 1998, Blair, like Clinton in the US, was able to maintain his electoral success because he pursued policies that were fundamentally at odds with the traditional policies of his party. He retained most of Thatcher's legislation restricting labor union activities, introduced substantial "market-oriented reforms" in the education and health sectors, which limited an increase in, or even reduced, government expenditure in these sectors, and reduced payments in various welfare programs.

During Blair's term in office (1997–2007), the economy's growth was aided in part by a steady inflow of foreign capital, but in 2008 the growth rate plummeted to minus 3.79 percent, due to the sudden decline in foreign direct investment that was the direct effect of the global financial crisis. Net foreign investment into the UK in 2009 fell to £30 billion, down from £91 billion in 2008, a drop of 67 percent.

Italy

The Italian economy fared even worse than the French and British economies during the period 1980–2008. During the first half of the 1980s, when Italy had three prime ministers in five years, its economy grew at an average rate of just 0.5 percent. It suffered from rapid inflation, a very high annual budget deficit of as much as 10 percent of GDP and a weak lira. The unemployment rate in these years averaged 12.5 percent. But, by the mid-1980s, successive administrations, which were essentially pursuing small government policies, had reduced both the budget deficit and inflation and stabilized the lira. However, these policies, pursued at the cost of neglecting investment to meet societal needs, were able to achieve an average growth rate of only 2 percent until the early 1990s.

But even this low growth rate could not be sustained after the early 1990s. From 1991 to 2007 the average annual growth rate fell to just 1.06 percent. And during these years Italy had four administrations, each of which had to struggle with an increasing deficit, declining exports and high rates of inflation and unemployment. Reducing the fiscal deficit during the late 1990s to below 3 percent of GDP in order to qualify as a eurozone member could not help but lower the growth rate. In 2008 the growth rate was minus 0.1 percent; it then plummeted to minus 5.1 percent in 2009.

Spain

In sharp contrast to Italy, Spain had the highest economic performance among the four countries from the 1980s to 2007. Although its GDP contracted by 0.2 percent in 1981, the economy continued to grow at an increasing rate during the 1980s, to achieve an average growth rate for the decade of 3.07 percent. Essentially, this was the result of the forceful policies adopted by the government of Felipe Gonzalez (1986–96) of the Spanish Socialist Party. Even though he had to pursue a fiscal policy of austerity in order to tame inflation, his policies succeeded because they included various policies to help industrial modernization, to privatize state-owned firms and to liberalize the labor market. Gonzalez achieved all of this despite the opposition of many in his own party. These and other equally non-socialistic policies gradually reduced Spain's high inflation, high unemployment and large trade deficit.

After a two-year recession in the early 1990s, the Spanish economy grew at an average rate of 3.29 percent until 2007. The principal reason for this performance was a vigorous real estate boom that was abetted by the Spanish banks' ability to make low-cost loans to homebuyers and property speculators. The banks were able to make these loans because they were in the eurozone and were thus able to borrow money readily at favorable real rates in the international capital market. But then the economy contracted by 3.75 percent in 2009 because the real estate bubble burst abruptly in 2008, and because of the financial crisis of 2007–08.

The economic performance and political developments during the period 1980–2008 in the four countries examined here leave us in no doubt of the following: these countries were generally adopting pro-investment policies, the most blatant of which was Thatcherism, because policymakers and voters, like their counterparts in the three largest developed economies, were unaware that they were living in the new world of necessary luxuries, in which pro-investment policies are futile.

From 2009 to the present

Following the financial crisis of 2007–08, the eurozone faced a currency crisis. This resulted from the crises of sovereign debt and of the financial institutions that began in 2009 in Greece, Ireland and Portugal. Simply stated, the crises were essentially a result of these countries' having experienced asset bubbles in the years leading up to the Great Recession. The global recession caused the bubbles to burst, forcing policymakers to increase deficit-financed public spending, and this in turn further increased the already high debt to GDP ratios. The amount of non-performing loans skyrocketed, thus causing massive bank losses and the bankruptcies of many banks and other financial institutions.

Confronted with the effects of the Great Recession and the eurozone crisis, all four economies continued to pursue ineffective pro-investment policies and thus grew at less than 1 percent per year in 2009 and 2010. Moreover, all four economies have grown only slowly since 2011 because they have continued to follow the misguided austerity policy of small government, which, like the pro-investment fiscal and monetary policies, is based on supply-side economics. The following summaries of widely known developments in these economies during the past several years provide evidence that what is urgently needed in each of these countries is for leaders and voters to realize that they are now living in a new world of too much stuff and they must make a systemic change to enable their capitalism and democracies to thrive into the future.

France

In France, Socialist Party President François Hollande compromised his political ideology and made a virtual U-turn in his policies because he became desperate. With the economy growing very sluggishly, the unemployment rate rising steadily and his approval rating plummeting, he was forced to try the very policies of supply-side economics that he had derided during his campaign for the presidency in 2012. The U-turn, which surprised and angered many in his own party, included breaking his 2012 campaign promises to impose higher taxes on the rich and to adopt several pro-labor policies. In order to pursue this U-turn, in September 2014 he had to dismiss three cabinet members who were objecting vigorously to his adoption of an austerity policy and pro-business tax policies. One of those dismissed from the cabinet was Minister of the Economy Arnaud Montebourg, who said:

> The austerity policy of reducing public spending decided by the government is the cause of the useless prolongation and aggravation of the economic crisis and the unnecessary suffering of citizens.[1]

In 2014, Hollande's government adopted a pro-investment policy that reduced taxes on companies in the amount of €40 billion. This was in exchange for a pledge by business to increase jobs by 500,000 within three years. The government increased VAT from 19.6 to 20 percent. It also adopted several other measures, such as reducing welfare payments for the poor, in order to pursue its fiscal austerity policy.[2] In September 2014 Hollande's government narrowly survived a vote of confidence by 269 to 244, because of the defection of 41 MPs from his own Socialist Party who strongly opposed the government's continuing pursuit of its version of supply-side economic policies.

Because of Hollande's policies, by the end of 2014 the number of the unemployed in France had risen to a record high of 3.5 million, or 9.9 percent. The economy continues to stagnate and grew only 1.1 percent in 2015. In April 2016, Hollande's popularity rating was down to 12 percent and mass media surveys showed that the likelihood of his becoming his party's candidate for the presidency in the 2017 election is slim, at best. Should he run again, it is likely he won't survive to the second round of the election because he will be defeated in the first round by Marine Le Pen of the Front National, the rightwing populist and xenophobic party.

The UK

In the UK, the conservative coalition government of the Conservative and Liberal Democratic parties took power as the result of 2010 election and initiated a five-year austerity program aimed at reducing the budget deficit from over 10 percent of GDP to 1 percent by 2015. To achieve this goal, under many guises the government vigorously reduced expenditure on welfare, national health, education and other areas, at the cost of inciting frequent protest marches and even social unrest. The main corporate tax rate paid by larger firms was steadily reduced, from 28 percent in 2010 to 24 percent in 2012, to 23 percent in 2013 and to 21 percent in 2014, while VAT was raised from 17.5 percent to 20 percent in 2011.

The inevitable consequence of these policies was a widening of the disparity in incomes, which was becoming apparent in many ways. Real average earnings have continued to decline since 2008. In 2014, a record high of 5.2 million workers were earning less than two-thirds of the median hourly pay because the number of higher-paying jobs in the manufacturing and financial industries had declined at the same time as the number of low-paying jobs in the service industries was rising. Also in 2014, the minimum wage set by the government rose by just 19 pence, to £6.50 per hour, while the living wage, calculated by the Living Wage Foundation, was higher, at £7.65 (£8.80 in London). The pay gap between British workers and the chief executives of large British firms has widened sharply; CEOs received 47 times the annual earnings of workers in 1998, but 133 times in 2014.[3]

The following quotation taken from the *Guardian*, a national center-left newspaper, on December 28, 2014 highlights some of the consequences of the policies adopted since 2011. The explanations in brackets are added for those readers who may not be familiar with British politics.

> The Liberal Democrats [in the coalition government] have made their boldest step yet to distance themselves from Conservative economic policy when David Laws [of the Liberal Democratic Party], a former deputy to George Osborne [the Chancellor

of Exchequer, i.e., the Minister of Finance] described the chancellor's public spending plans to 2020 as a political suicide note. They were so severe, he said, that they made Thatcherism look like a policy devised by Tony Benn [a prominent figure in the Labour Party and a cabinet minister in the 1970s, well known for his strong leftwing views].

Laws said the Conservatives made a politically catastrophic error in trying to draw up rightwing economic dividing lines that will require cuts in some Whitehall departments [the principal ministries, located on or near the road in London named Whitehall] of a quarter. Conservative voters who value the armed forces, police and prisons will be worried by the "mind-boggling" consequences of the cuts, Laws said.

Even then the Conservatives will only achieve their goals if they find welfare cuts on a scale that would hugely increase the levels of poverty in the country.

The Liberal Democrats have signed up to clearing the deficit in day-to-day spending in 2017–18. But they say this must be achieved by some tax rises, and not, as does the Conservatives plan, only through spending cuts. Nick Clegg's party does not support the 2 billion pounds of welfare cuts proposed by Osborne in the first two years of the parliament. [Nick Clegg was then the leader of the Liberal Democratic Party.]

Because of the stringent fiscal austerity policy and other policies that were increasing poverty, the British economy managed to grow by only 2.6 percent in 2014 and it is not at all likely that it will be able to sustain even this performance in the coming years. However, because of the strength of the conservative narrative based on supply-side economics, the Conservative Party won a majority in the election of May 2015.

A significant outcome of this election was the election of Jeremy Corbyn as the new leader of the Labour Party. Corbyn was a backbencher, long known for his staunch socialist views, which are leftwing even within the Labour Party. He advocates many policies that reflect the traditional policies of the Labour Party, such as the renationalization of public utilities and the railways, increasing the social safety net, raising the effective tax rates on the wealthy and on corporations and making more societal investments. However, unlike Blair and Clinton, who succeeded in winning elections by compromising the traditional values of their respective parties, the likelihood of the Corbyn-led Labour Party's compromising its values and winning the next election is extremely low.

Given the strength of the conservative narrative, the Conservative Party will continue to rule by beguiling the electorate. This means that the current pro-investment policies and fiscal austerity will continue and, as a result, the British economy will remain in a secular stagnation and suffer the consequences.

Italy

Next we turn to Italy. The Italian government bond rate was 4 percent in November 2010 but rose steadily, to reach 7.1 percent by August 2012, putting Italy into a financial crisis. This was the inevitable result of the policies both of the profligate conservative government of Silvio Berlusconi, who served as prime minister during the years 1994–95, 2001–05 and 2008–11, and of the center-left governments of the intervening years, which accumulated the national debt by continuing deficit-financed, vote-getting policies.

In the wake of the debt crisis, Mario Monti, an economist, became prime minister in November 2011. His government was a "technocratic" government, that is, it mostly consisted of skilled technical specialists trained in economics. His administration immediately adopted emergency austerity measures in order to regain the confidence of the international financial market. Although his government was unable to prevent the crisis of the government bond rate rising steeply by 2012, it did succeed in stabilizing the bond rate and passed a few laws intended to revitalize the sluggish economy (for example, one law relaxed a few of the most stringent employment practices). But the austerity policy kept the Italian economy stagnant, growing at a rate of only 0.5 percent in 2012 and 2013.

The election in 2013 replaced the Monti government, putting into power a center-left grand coalition government headed by Enrico Letta. But Letta's tenure lasted only from July 2013 to February 2014, when his leftwing rival Matteo Renzi, the leader of the Democratic Party, withdrew his party's support for the grand coalition. Renzi disagreed with Letta's policies, blaming Letta for the ongoing fiscal crisis and recession.

Renzi succeeded in forming a government, becoming the youngest prime minister in the history of Italy. His rise to power is widely seen as a sign that Italians recognize the need for fundamental change in their political and economic institutions and practices. By the end of 2015, Renzi had succeeded in making a few very significant changes: he weakened the power of the Senate, which often obstructed the enactment of nationally necessary policies for the sake of regional and other interests of the Senators; made the labor market more flexible; downsized the bureaucracy; and improved the civil justice system. Meanwhile, the Italian economy continues to grow at less than 1 per cent because, like all other developed economies, what is needed is a systemic change to enable Italy to adopt new fiscal and monetary policies.

Renzi has indicated his awareness of the serious flaws of a fiscal austerity policy:

> We cannot go on reasoning only on the basis of austerity and rigor. In a phase of deflation and stagnation, we can't. We have to keep our accounts in order, spend money well, yes, because Germany is preoccupied that southern countries don't spend money wisely – and it's true – but the central point is that if we tackle our problems, European economics must change in favor of investment in growth.[4]

Renzi is very much aware that Europe must make investments for growth, but he is still thinking "inside the box." He hasn't realized that the investments that must be made in the new world of necessary luxuries are those that meet the needs of society, which will become possible only after a systemic change is made in the existing capitalist system.

Thus, so long as no systemic change is made, the future of Italy will continue to be bleak, as aptly described by *The Economist*:

> Since the financial crisis, two recessions have sent Italian industrial firms reeling ... Last year, just 397,000 cars rolled off domestic assembly lines at Fiat, Italy's largest carmaker, against 911,000 in 2007. [...]
>
> The crisis has served to highlight systemic weaknesses in Italy. [...] The only way to survive weak demand and growing competition [...] is to shift production to lower-cost countries, as Italian makers are now doing. [...]
>
> Slumping output at producers of cars and kitchen gadgets has devastated those who make parts for them. Many have already gone bust. [...]
>
> [...] For the foreseeable future Italian manufacturers are stuck trying to sell their existing products to consumers who seem in no rush to replace their old bangers and creaking kitchen gadgets. In a climate of political and economic uncertainty, [...] who can blame them for that?[5]

Spain

Like France, the UK and Italy, Spain too has continued to adopt pro-investment policies and so remains trapped in a secular stagnation. The Spanish government was forced to seek €100 billion from the EU and the IMF in 2012 in order to bail out its banking system. Many industries in Spain have become less competitive internationally, and so Spain has had an annual trade deficit, resulting in a stagnating economy since 2008.

Spain limps from one recession to the next, which has sharply increased the rate of unemployment, which reached 24.4 percent by the end of 2009, and then 27.4 percent by 2013. Unemployment among youth aged under 25 rose at twice the rate for all workers, standing at 53 percent in 2013. As a result, more and more of the young have become alienated from politics, as can be seen in their plummeting participation in elections. Youth now lead the separatist movement of Catalonia and several thousand per year emigrate to wherever they can find jobs.

In 2011, José Zapatero, the socialist prime minister since 2004, was replaced by Mariano Rajoy of the conservative People's Party. Rajoy won mainly because he promised the revival of the economy through the adoption of pro-investment policies. He pursued harsh austerity measures and adopted a new labor law in early 2012. These brought about two general strikes during the same year. The financial scandals of his senior party officials have further eroded his government's approval rating. Although the Spanish economy performed a little better than the economies of France and Italy during 2015, the budget deficit was still 4.2 percent of GDP and the debt to GDP ratio exceeded 100 percent.

The following excerpt from the *Guardian* on April 30, 2012 provides a glimpse of the reality of the Spanish economy and politics of recent years.

> In Spain, thousands protested against spending cuts introduced by Prime Minister Mariano Rajoy's conservative government. The cuts, being particularly severely felt in the education and healthcare sectors, are aimed at tackling a debt crisis that has pushed the country back into recession and driven unemployment close to 25%.
>
> [...]
>
> Protesters in northeastern Barcelona, northern Bilbao, eastern Valencia and many other regional capitals carried banners urging Rajoy not to "mess around with health and education." Labour unions called for large-scale protests to continue in coming months to persuade Rajoy and regional governments to implement measures to stimulate growth.
>
> [...]

The ILO [International Labor Organization] said it was concerned at the way young people were being shut out of labour markets and the rise of short-term contracts, which also hit the young and women more than other groups.

"Four years into the global crisis, labour market imbalances are becoming more structural, and therefore more difficult to eradicate. Certain groups, such as the long-term unemployed, are at risk of exclusion from the labour market. This means that they would be unable to obtain new employment even if there were a strong recovery."[6]

In 2014 the populist Podemos Party was formed. Podemos means "We Can" in Spanish, and this party seeks to reduce economic disparity, unemployment and corruption in Spanish politics. The following excerpt gives a sense of the political mood of Spain, and also of a large number of citizens in all of Western Europe.

Tens of thousands of people have massed in central Madrid for a rally organized by radical Spanish leftists Podemos.

The "March for Change" is one of the party's first outdoor mass rallies, as it looks to build on the recent victory of its close allies Syriza in Greece.

Podemos has surged into the lead in recent opinion polls, and says it will seek to write off part of Spain's debt if it wins elections later this year.

Podemos says politicians should "serve the people, not private interests."

[...]

Podemos leader Pablo Iglesias spelt out the party's message to the crowd.

"We want change," he said [...]. "I know that governing is difficult but those who have serious dreams can change things."[6]

As of the end of April 2016, Spain still does not have a government, exposing the deep ideological schism in the country. As a result of the election of December 20, 2015, neither Prime Minister Rajoy's party nor the Socialist Party could form a government. Despite the continuing efforts of both parties, neither could agree to the terms necessary to get the support of the Podemos Party or the Ciudadanos, the Citizens Party, a left-of-center party founded in Catalonia. (The election outcome was People's Party, 123, Socialists, 90, Podemos, 42, Ciudadanos, 40, and six minor parties, 28.) Meanwhile, the prospects for the Spanish economy in 2016 remain far from hopeful. Unemployment exceeds 20 percent and the continuing political impasse increases the uncertainty that is affecting the economy.

Conclusion

The post-1980 history of the seven countries surveyed in this and the preceding chapters should tell us the following: the pro-investment policies and a smaller government policy that conservative governments have adopted and that liberal governments were forced to adopt because of the political strength of the conservative narrative don't work. The experience of the past several decades has shown that all the policies based on supply-side economics have not only been futile in invigorating economies in our new world, they have also had numerous negative consequences. The most momentous among them are the increasing Gini coefficients that threaten democracy, and the production of more necessary luxuries at the cost of further degrading the environment.

ELEVEN

Reform to
the rescue

Since the Industrial Revolution began in the mid–18th century, the capitalist system has made two successful systemic changes. The first occurred in Britain in the mid–19th century, and the second in the US between the 1890s and 1930s. This chapter presents a very brief summary of the substance of both systemic changes, which were made by overcoming formidable and entrenched opposition.

Great Britain[1]

England gave birth to the Industrial Revolution in the 1760s, and by the 1830s and 1840s the British system faced increasing political and economic problems that threatened the very system itself.

The most important threat was the huge disparity in income and wealth created by the Industrial Revolution. By the first decades of the 19th century, almost 30 percent of England's population was living in abject poverty in urban slums. Most slum dwellers could not afford even such basic necessities as a sufficient amount of food. Families lived in unventilated, overcrowded and inadequately heated two-room apartments with few or no sanitation facilities. Poor sanitation led to frequent typhoid and cholera epidemics. Major outbreaks of cholera occurred in English cities in 1831–32 and in 1848–49.

The former was more widespread than the latter, claiming the lives of more than 52,000 people.

Although England and Wales had several centuries of experience with the Poor Laws, the authorities were not at all equipped to deal with such widespread, appalling poverty. This led the Whig Party to pass the Poor Law Amendment Act in 1834, forcing those poor who were in receipt of poor relief to live and work in workhouses, even if it meant splitting up families. Forcing people to perform assigned work in exchange for shelter and a meager diet did little to mitigate the rampant poverty.

A no less important threat to the system was the increasing inefficiency of the British economy by the 1830s. The mercantilist system that had prevailed since the 17th century protected the economy from foreign competition for the purpose of increasing the political and economic power of the nation at the expense of rival nations. The mercantilist goal was pursued through the imposition of tariffs that had the effect of reducing imports and protected the interests of politically powerful aristocratic landowners and industrialists. By the beginning of the 19th century the list of goods protected by tariffs exceeded a thousand items. The most notorious tariffs were those imposed on all cereal products by the Corn Laws, which were first enacted in 1815 and remained in place until 1846. These tariffs benefited rich landowners at the expense of making the lives of urban workers and the poor unendurable.

By the mid-19th century, even the severely circumscribed democracy of the time had become dysfunctional. The most significant manifestation of this was the "rotten boroughs," electoral districts of the House of Commons that had very small numbers of voters and were controlled by aristocratic landowners. To counter the mounting criticism, the House of Commons passed the First Reform Act of 1832, which removed parliamentary seats from the rotten boroughs and created seats in the new industrial towns, thus ending the most obvious defects of the 18th-century political system. However, political power remained firmly in the hands of the gentry, the aristocracy and the wealthy industrialists. A majority of the population, including all women, still had no vote.

Added to these problems, Britain was in a dire fiscal plight during most of the first half of the 19th century. Chancellors of the exchequer issued annual budgets to meet only short-term needs and borrowed their way out of difficulties, with no clear vision for how to achieve long-term fiscal stability. In the absence of a coherent, long-term fiscal policy, Britain's fiscal condition remained precarious. By 1840 debt servicing was taking up 58 percent of all public revenues, leaving 25 percent for national defense and a meager 17 percent for everything else. This situation was remarkably similar to that of France in 1788, when the state fell into bankruptcy and the French Revolution erupted in the following year.

Britain managed to avoid a political revolution because it succeeded in changing its system, although it took nearly half a century of slow and steady efforts to accomplish this. Many of the reforms were achieved because an increasing number of politicians became convinced of their necessity. However, few historians would disagree that a crucial, if not the decisive, role in the success of the systemic change was played by William Ewart Gladstone (1809–98), who served as chancellor of the exchequer four times between 1853 and 1882 and as prime minister four times (1868–74, 1880–85, February–July 1886 and 1892–94).

Gladstone was first elected to Parliament in 1832 as a Tory and held junior offices in Robert Peel's government during 1834 and 1835. But he steadily moved towards liberalism. Even though he had entered Peel's Conservative cabinet in 1838, when the Conservatives split in 1846 he followed Peel in becoming a Liberal-Conservative. In 1859, he and other Peelites merged with the Whigs and the Radicals to form the Liberal Party, and he became its leader in 1867. Gladstone became popular with working people because of his support for electoral reform and his role in abolishing the Corn Laws while he was still a member of Peel's Conservative cabinet. For what he had done while he was a Conservative, and later as the leader of Liberal Party, he earned the nickname the "People's William."

However, the success of the systemic change, which not only forestalled a possible revolution but enabled Britain to build an empire, would not have been possible without the concerted effort of the Liberal Party and its success in overcoming the opposition of the conservative Tory Party. The reforms that the Liberals incrementally pushed through the House of Commons had the result of altering the economic and power relationships within British society.

The repeal of the Corn Laws in 1846 was very important, vastly improving conditions for the poorest in society because it immediately lowered the price of bread. Indeed, some historians believe this probably saved Britain from a French-style revolution. Then, in 1858, the Workhouse Visiting Society was formed to inspect conditions in workhouses, and during the mid-1860s major laws were enacted to require parishes to share with the government more of the costs of aiding the poor. Because of such efforts on the part of the government, the needs of the poor were better served and their numbers living in workhouses were reduced.

Other legislative changes that would have been inconceivable at the beginning of the 19th century were made between the 1830s and 1870s. The Mills and Factories Act of 1833 limited the employment hours of children under the age of 18, required various improvements in working conditions, forbade night work for children under the age of 18 and provided for inspectors to enforce the law. The Labour in Factories Act of 1844 extended children's working-hours protection to women, strengthened the authority of inspectors and introduced safety regulations. The Coal Mines Regulation Act of 1872 required mines to employ state-certified managers who were capable of dealing with numerous safety, health and other issues. These are just a sample of the labor laws that passed by Parliament during the 19th century.

As chancellor of the exchequer, Gladstone had the first balanced annual budget approved by the House of Commons in April 1853. Although the budget was for only a single year, it established the principle that all expenditure, including war finance, had to be paid for by raising taxes. Most of the needed tax revenues were paid by the wealthy property owners. In order to be able to adopt this first balanced budget, Gladstone had to debate for a total of 15 hours in five separate meetings to win support for it within his own cabinet. However mundane a balanced budget may sound to us today, this was a historic achievement that laid the foundation for Britain's fiscal strength. It enabled the British government to cope with the demands of the Crimean War (1853–56) without resorting to large-scale borrowing, in sharp contrast to France and Russia, where the war almost crippled the finances of both countries. Some historians believe Gladstone's success in getting this first budget approved cemented his reputation as an extraordinary statesman who enabled the British democratic capitalist system to survive.

In addition to inaugurating annual, balanced budgets and carrying out various other fiscal reforms, Gladstone pressed ahead with electoral reform. The Second Reform Act of 1867 doubled the numbers of the electorate, while the Secret Ballot Act of 1872 helped to minimize the lingering traces of corruption and the influence of the aristocrats and the wealthy on elections. In 1884, the Third Reform Act increased the electorate to 5 million males, thereby very significantly diminishing the political power of the landowning gentry, the aristocrats and the industrialists.

By the norms of the 21st century, British capitalist democracy at the end of the 19th century was still seriously flawed in many significant respects. But the legacy of Gladstone, the Liberal Party and other reformers was a political–economic system that was substantively different from the system that had been in place at the beginning of the 19th century. Had it not been for this systemic change, Great Britain could have had a revolution and would not have remained a model of democracy and capitalism.

The United States[2]

American systemic change was achieved because of the Progressive Movement that began during the 1890s and grew in strength to the end of the First World War, and then through the reforms that were made during the Great Depression of the 1930s.

The Progressive Movement was launched in response to many grave social ills and the pervasive political corruption that rapid industrialization since the mid-19th century had brought to American capitalist democracy. By the 1890s, the United States was characterized by a widening chasm in the distribution of income and wealth; by excessive political and economic power held by the industrialists (often referred to as the "robber barons") and their henchmen, who endangered the health and welfare of citizens; by the widespread rigging of elections; by the suppression of labor unions; plus many other manifestations of unbridled capitalism and dysfunctional democracy.

By the final few decades of the 19th century, the population of American cities was growing at a dramatic rate. This was primarily due to the expansion of industry and the arrival of immigrants – mainly from Europe – along with a steady stream of people coming from the rural regions. Industrial expansion and population growth radically changed American cities. Slums with overcrowded tenement houses with minimum sanitation facilities proliferated. Many urban dwellers, and especially the slum dwellers, suffered from appalling poverty. But government was controlled by the wealthy and the corrupt. It did little to provide safety nets, despite the fact that a prolonged depression of the economy between the financial panics of 1893 and 1897 increased unemployment to between 10 and 14 percent.

This was the background to the emergence of the Progressive Movement during the 1890s. It started locally, led by civic leaders from various professional groups, such as educators and the clergy. As more national leaders of religious groups, educational institutions and businesses joined, the movement gradually became national. It steadily won support at the highest political levels, including from Presidents Theodore Roosevelt and Woodrow Wilson and many leading politicians. Originally sparked by the anger and desperation of citizens, the movement demanded greater democracy, more social justice, an uncorrupt government effective in regulating business, improved working conditions and a reduction in the horrendously unequal distribution of income and wealth.

The Progressive Movement was effectively aided by many writers and journalists who published trenchant, often investigative, articles and books that excoriated the greed and anti-social conduct of many in high finance, food-related industries, the railroad and many other businesses. The best known among these publications are Ida Tarbell's *The History of the Standard Oil Company*, which exposed the greed-driven, monopolistic behavior of the oil firm; Upton Sinclair's *The Jungle*, which exposed the unsanitary conditions in the large Chicago meat-packing firms; and Theodore Dreiser's *The Financier* and *The Titan*, which were written in such a way that laymen could understand the unethical machinations of financial institutions and big business. The term "The Gilded Age," referring to the period from the 1870s to the turn of the century, came from the title of a book written by Mark Twain and Charles Warner, who satirized the era when many grave socio-economic and political problems were "gilded" over so that they could be concealed.

The movement led to changes that were so fundamental that even its strongest supporters could not have imagined them possible when the movement began. These included three amendments to the Constitution: the 16th, which imposed an income tax; the 17th, which changed the election of senators to popular vote instead of by state legislatures; and the 19th, which gave women the vote. In addition, the following laws were enacted: the Interstate Commerce Act of 1887, which regulated the railroads; the Federal Reserve Act of 1913, which established the Federal Reserve Bank; and three antitrust laws (Sherman, 1890; Clayton, 1916; and the Federal Trade Commission, 1916). In addition, Congress passed the Meat Inspection Act, the Pure Food and Drug Act and several laws relating to workers' compensation and child labor. All of these amendments and laws effected a sea-change in the capitalist democratic system of the time and helped to transform the system into one that was much more inclusive and transparent.

Still, many serious problems remained. The most important were a huge disparity in the distribution of income and wealth and the virtual absence of tax-funded safety nets. Prior to the First World War, there was only a very low income tax rate (1 to 6 percent of net income) and this was paid by an extremely small number of the wealthiest taxpayers, thus leaving the government with a woefully inadequate amount of tax revenue to provide safety nets and meet all other social needs. The income tax rate rose only slowly during the 1920s, resulting in very little change in the distribution of income and wealth during the decade. Moreover, the enforcement of antitrust and other laws continued to be far from effectual because of persistent political corruption and the suppression of the labor union movement. Banks and wealthy investors continued to engage in various unethical and increasingly risky practices and investments, and the prices of stocks continued to rise during the 1920s, making the rich even richer.

A high rate of immigration and the suppression of union activities kept wages from rising. The result was a still steadily rising disparity in income and wealth. This provided the backdrop to F. Scott Fitzgerald's 1925 novel *The Great Gatsby*, with its themes of the wealthy resisting social change and maintaining their decadent lifestyles. The huge inequality in the distribution of income and wealth continued to the onset of the Great Depression.

The Great Depression began in the US in October 1929. There were several complex, interlinked causes for the Depression, such as the decline in demand, due to the income and wealth disparity that had increased during the 1920s, and, as occurred in all of the developed capitalist economies, both the deteriorating stability of financial institutions and the adoption of misguided monetary policies. But what triggered the Depression was the bursting of the stock market bubble of the 1920s. The bubble had been abetted by increasingly risky speculative trading and had to burst sooner or later. The effects were devastating. Wages, prices, profits and tax revenues all plunged. The unemployment rate shot up to 25 percent, leaving millions of workers destitute because no government-funded real safety net was available. Although demand for goods and services declined steadily, the government reduced its expenditure and the Federal Reserve Bank did little to stimulate the economy. Between 1929 and 1932, total industrial output declined by one third.

President Herbert Hoover lost the 1932 election to Franklin D. Roosevelt by a landslide. Roosevelt initiated the New Deal, which consisted of numerous programs and newly enacted laws that substantially expanded the roles of the government and collectively helped the US to complete a systemic change. Many of the programs adopted were unprecedented. These included the Civilian Conservation Corps, created in 1933, and the Works Progress Administration, begun in 1935. The former provided jobs for over 3 million men to engage in conservation and the development of parks, rivers and many other natural resources in rural lands owned by federal, state and local governments. The latter employed almost 8 million people to construct public buildings, roads and many other types of public facilities and to engage in a wide variety of culture-related projects, even paying musicians to play in opera performances and concerts.

The laws enacted substantively aided in reshaping American capitalism. The most significant included the Glass–Steagall Act of 1933, which restricted the highly risky but very profitable investment activities of financial institutions; the Wagner Act of 1933, which guaranteed the basic rights of private sector employees to organize trade unions and engage in collective bargaining and strikes; and several laws enacted during 1935 and 1936 which established the social security system, aimed at minimizing poverty and destitution.

It took half a century, from the 1890s to the 1930s and the Great Depression, to change the American system. But the change enabled the US to achieve economic prosperity and emerge as the undisputed global political and economic power after the Second World War.

TWELVE

Adapting capitalism and changing politics

Capitalism succeeded in large part because it adapted. Capitalism is not a blank slate upon which anything can be written: it has a central core that must be preserved if it is to remain capitalism ... Capitalism has to change from time to time if capitalism is to survive.

—Herbert Stein,
Essays on Economics, Economists and Politics (American Enterprise Institute, 2004), pp. 27–8[1]

Introduction

Because we have failed to realize that we are now in the new world of necessary luxuries, since the 1980s all the developed economies have been committing the great folly of adopting futile pro-investment policies based on supply-side economics and striving to make government ever smaller. As the preceding chapters have demonstrated, this is folly because these economies are continuing to suffer from all the consequences of the ongoing secular economic stagnation; that is, they are failing to provide adequate safety nets and to invest in what is necessary to meet the needs of society. No less important, this folly has undermined democracy by widening the disparity in the distribution of income and wealth. However, there is no need to continue committing this folly, because we have the ability to change the existing democratic capitalist system and make these economies grow robustly once again and become much more egalitarian.

In order to show how a third systemic change of capitalism can be made in our new world, the first section of this chapter discusses the following: (1) how to increase the tax revenues that are essential to simultaneously achieve the goals of making the investment to meet societal needs and increase the demand necessary to enable the economy to grow; (2) some of the major examples of changes to be made in economic institutions and practices; and (3) a few of the most important examples of changes that need to be made in political institutions and practices. The discussions will be presented only for the US, Japan and Germany, but can serve as useful examples for other developed economies.

Next, the chapter puts forth the following two arguments: first, a "larger government" does not mean that the system will change from capitalist to socialist. The argument that a larger government will result in socialism (or even Marxist socialism) is based on ideologically motivated and erroneous definitions of socialism. Second, the belief that capitalism cannot coexist with an egalitarian democracy is wrong for two reasons. The historical trend of the last few centuries shows that capitalist economies have coexisted with democracy even at times when systemic change was undertaken, as occurred in the UK and the US.

The chapter ends with the following argument: to be more productively efficient, capitalist economies need to grow. However, the growth rate should be measured not only by the rate of growth of the quantity of goods and services produced but also by the qualitative change that improves the quality of life for ourselves and future generations, that is, by better meeting societal needs, including averting the looming environmental catastrophe.

Increasing tax revenues

Since voters in each country need to debate and decide on the amount by which tax revenues should be increased in order to begin the third systemic change, here I shall confine myself to offering only what I believe to be a useful basis upon which to begin the debate. For reasons that will become clear, I suggest that the discussion should begin with an increase in tax revenues of 5 percent of GDP. This increase would keep the ratio of total tax revenues to GDP in all of the developed economies significantly lower than it was prior to the 1980s. This would make it possible to substantially increase investment to meet societal needs in order to increase demand necessary for raising the growth rate of the economy and reduce disparities in the distribution of income and wealth.

The US

First, let us consider the US, where 5 percent of GDP is about $1 trillion. Based on data presented in Chapter Six on neglected investments and Chapter Seven on the United States, it can be reasonably argued that $1 trillion of additional tax revenue per year is the minimum necessary amount to meet societal needs and increase demand in order to help the American economy to begin to grow steadily at close to 3 per cent.

A significant proportion of $1 trillion could be obtained by increasing the income tax rates on the wealthy. In 2014, the Treasury Department and other organizations, such as the Tax Policy Center and the Brookings Institution, calculated how this could be done. The top 1 percent of income earners – about 1.13 million households each earning an average of $2.1 million – were paying federal income tax at just under 30 percent, and not at the highest marginal rate of 39.6 percent. This was because dividends and capital gains are taxed at only 15 percent and because there are numerous other clauses in US tax law that make tax avoidance possible.

If the effective tax rate on the top 1 percent were raised to 45 percent, it would increase total tax revenues by $276 billion, which is more than one quarter of the $1 trillion needed.

Estimates by the Treasury Department show that eliminating the preferential 15 percent tax rate on capital gains and dividends alone would generate $134 billion per year. Even if the top 1 percent paid taxes at 45 percent, their average annual post-tax incomes would still exceed $1 million. And if the effective tax rates on the top 5 percent, who each earned an average of $164,546 and paid income taxes at the effective rate of 20.46 percent in 2014, were raised to 30 percent, this would yield additional tax revenues of around $50 billion.

The tax on corporations, another major source of tax revenue, can also be raised. The effective rate of this tax has been declining even more than the nominal rate, which has been reduced since the 1980s. In 2014 this tax yielded $320 billion in revenue, or approximately 10.6 percent of the total tax revenues. In contrast, corporations were taxed at rates that yielded between 20 and 30 percent of the total tax revenues from the end of the Second World War to the end of the 1970s. If the effective rate of corporate tax were raised by 10 percent, this would yield an additional $30 billion, increasing the total revenue from this tax to $350 billion.

That is, the above-noted increases in the income tax rates for the top 1 percent and the top 5 percent and the corporate tax alone would yield additional tax revenue of $356 billion, well above one third of $1 trillion. Because the current pro-investment fiscal policy has been focused on reducing taxes, many other tax rates could be raised and new taxes could be levied to obtain the remaining necessary tax revenue to reach the desired $1 trillion. And it should be noted here that even had total tax revenues been raised by $1 trillion in 2015, the total tax to GDP ratio of the US would have increased from 26.9 percent to 31.9 percent – still below 34.9 percent, the average ratio of all 34 OECD economies in 2015.

Japan and Germany

Next, before discussing other taxes whose rates could be raised or that could be newly levied, let us briefly consider Japan and Germany. For Japan, an increase in tax revenues of 5 percent of GDP would yield about $250 billion, and for Germany, about $190 billion. Calculations made using the data of the ministries of finance in Japan and Germany and other respected economic research organizations in both countries leave little doubt as to the following: the income tax rate on the wealthy has fallen significantly in both countries since the 1980s. Thus, if the rate were raised by 5 percent on the top 5 percent of income earners, it would yield in Japan at least 26 percent of the tax increases needed to meet the goal of raising additional tax revenue by 5 percent of GDP. The same yield for Germany would be 22 percent.

Other taxes

There are almost limitless combinations of taxes that could be raised in order to obtain the needed amount of tax revenues. Thus, let us now look at only the most important taxes besides income and corporate taxes.

Wealth

Today, when the distribution of wealth has become so unequal, a wealth tax needs to be seriously considered. This tax could be imposed internationally. For example, Thomas Piketty proposed one for the EU: 1 percent for households with wealth of over €1 million but less than €5 million and 2 percent on wealth of over €5 million. He estimated that this tax would be paid by about 2.5 percent of households.[2]

There is no doubt that the probability of such a wealth tax being adopted internationally is extremely low because of the expected very strong opposition. However, the possibility of its being adopted in some form is not zero, for two main reasons. Since the late 1990s and especially after the Great Recession of 2007-08, at summit meetings of the EU and G8, the coordination of efforts to reduce tax avoidance and evasion by multinational firms has been seriously discussed, and more and more bilateral agreements to minimize evasion of income and corporate taxes have been reached. Also, disparity in the distribution of wealth has become an important political issue in all of the rich economies.

Admittedly, adopting a wealth tax on a national basis would face very strong opposition in all rich countries. But the opposition could not be stronger than when income tax was first introduced, or when income tax rates were raised significantly in the past. The debate will be time consuming and vehement. However, today, when the huge disparity in the distribution of wealth has become a critical political and social issue, time is on the side of the supporters of such a tax if it is carefully designed and preceded by intensive debate to obtain the support of a majority of voters.

Luxuries

Several other taxes, on which there is already a substantial literature and experience, are worthy of discussion. One is a well-designed tax on luxuries. All rich economies have either adopted such a tax in the past or are adopting one today. A judicious definition of luxury goods and services is needed, so that the categories of goods and services to be taxed will be supported by a majority of voters. Most importantly, this tax would help to protect the environment by reducing the use of resources to produce what many today believe are "necessary" luxury goods and services, even though by most rational standards they are not necessary. Most voters would agree to a list that included such luxuries as automobiles costing over $100,000, suites in luxury hotels, mega-mansions, yachts, expensive jewelry and gourmet meals at expensive restaurants.

Tobin tax

Another tax worthy of serious discussion is a tax on financial transactions. This was first proposed in 1972 by James Tobin, an American economist and Nobel laureate. The Tobin tax gained many supporters during the 1980s and 1990s when Mexico, Southeast Asia and Russia all faced financial crises that resulted in part from drastic fluctuations in the value of their currencies. The proposed Tobin tax was a tax of about 0.5 percent to be levied on "spot currency transactions" (in which each party promises to pay a certain amount of currency to the other on the same day or within a day or two). The purpose was to minimize those currency transactions that benefited speculators but played havoc with a number of economies. The Tobin tax has not yet been adopted by any country but it continues to be considered in most of the developed economies.

What could be adopted is a variant of the Tobin tax on transactions of currencies, stocks, bonds, derivatives and other financial instruments. The purposes of such a tax vary and include raising revenue, reducing disparity in the distribution of income and wealth and creating a fund to bail out financial institutions in the future. Various versions of this tax have been proposed in the EU and in the US, but because of effective opposition from politically powerful financial institutions and conservative political leaders few countries have adopted it. However, Sweden, France and Italy have all adopted a version of it. The Swedish tax, frequently cited as an example of a very poorly designed transaction tax on stocks and bonds, was imposed and subsequently abandoned during the 1980s. France and Italy adopted a version of this tax in 2012 and 2013, respectively, but in both cases the revenue raised is small because the tax is levied on very narrowly defined transactions and at a very low rate.

These examples, however, are useful in debating whether a tax on transactions of financial papers could be levied either internationally or within a single country. What is needed is an intensive debate on how to design an effective tax that would yield a sufficient amount of revenue, would be feasible to administer at least cost and would cause the least amount of distortion in the working of the capital market. Arguments have been advanced to date against various versions of the Tobin tax, such as the technical difficulties involved in designing the tax and a loss in the efficiency of use of capital. But these are no more valid than similar arguments made by the opponents of income tax, antitrust laws and other similarly ground-breaking legislation enacted during the first two systemic changes.

Environmental taxes

There are numerous other familiar possibilities for taxes that could raise the remainder of the needed tax revenue, and thus should be debated, such as inheritance and property taxes. However, here let us discuss what can be broadly termed environmental taxes. Although the US and Japan have adopted narrowly defined, minor environmental taxes relating to petroleum, many European and some other developed economies, either regionally (that is, within the EU) or within single countries, have adopted many forms of this kind of tax. These range from many versions of carbon-credit trading to taxes on the use of various natural resources (such as water, coal and petroleum). These taxes usually have the dual purpose of protecting the environment and raising revenue. They need to be carefully designed, considering their effects (such as on productive efficiency and possible regressive effects). Although various broadly defined environmental taxes are currently being levied, these taxes continue to face strong opposition and need to be debated more vigorously in order to design taxes that will protect the environment much more effectively and to raise an appropriate level of revenues.

The expected public response

What would be the likely public response to increases in taxes? Even if voters agreed on an initial tax increase to raise revenues by an equivalent of at least 5 percent of GDP, many voters could be expected to ask for how long the increased tax must be paid in order to make the societal investments needed to increase the economic growth rate. This question, however, is academic, for the following reason. A majority of voters, who would see an increase in the growth rate of the economy and the beneficial effects of tax-funded investments to meet vital societal needs, would most likely vote to maintain the larger tax revenues, or even vote for larger increase in tax revenues, exceeding 5 percent of GDP. I believe it is reasonable to expect that most of those individuals who at first objected strenuously to an increased tax burden would think as follows once they saw the results:

> "It is becoming very obvious that the increased tax-funded investments to meet the needs of society today and into the future that we are now able to make are reinvigorating the economy. Profits and dividends, the prices of stocks and other assets are now increasing because they are primarily determined by the growth rate of the economy, which began to increase because of the tax-funded investments. And, most important, we are now beginning to reduce the risks to democracy by starting to rectify the wide economic disparity, because employment and real wages are rising, thanks to the higher growth rate of the economy.
>
> "Although of course I would prefer lower taxes, the recent tax increase is turning out to be advantageous for everyone, unlike the ineffective pro-investment policy that many of us supported because of its tempting narrative of reducing taxes to benefit everyone. Yes, after seeing what the tax increase has done, the current tax-funded societal investments must remain in place or should even be increased. Paying higher taxes is definitely preferable to continuing to suffer all the consequences of slow economic growth, which include a possible drastic political change, which would be more than likely to reduce my income and wealth much more than the higher taxes I am now paying."

Political change

In order to make a third systemic change possible, it is as important to change political institutions and practices as it is to change tax laws. Needless to say, this will be a complex undertaking that will encounter fierce opposition. The following suggests only a few of the most important examples of changes that need to be debated in the US, Japan and Germany.

The US

In the US, "safe" gerrymandered electoral districts must be eliminated. Gerrymandering is a practice that attempts to establish a political advantage for a particular party by manipulating electoral district boundaries. The practice is named after Governor Elbridge Gerry of Massachusetts, who signed a Bill in 1812 that redistricted the state to the advantage of his Democratic Republican Party, the conservative party of his era. Currently, as many as 85 to 90 percent of the electoral districts for the House of Representatives decidedly favor a candidate of one party. This increases the likelihood of an ideologically more left-leaning candidate being elected in Democratic districts, or a more right-leaning candidate in Republican districts. The result is an increase in the fiercely ideologically based legislative confrontations that have made it extremely difficult to deal with many important issues facing the country. As was discussed in Chapter Seven, this is the reason why in recent decades the US legislature has become gridlocked to the point of having extreme difficulty in agreeing on an annual budget, thus causing the government to be shut down.

Another very important change that must be made is to find ways to reverse two Supreme Court decisions discussed in Chapter Seven. One eliminated the limits on financial contributions to political action committees (organizations that pool campaign contributions from donors in order to campaign for or against candidates, ballot initiatives or legislation). The second significantly increased the amount of funds that an individual can donate to a political candidate. Both of these decisions were based on the profoundly mistaken ground that such contributions are an expression of the freedom of speech guaranteed by the Constitution.

Japan

In Japan, the egregious differences in weight of votes in different electoral districts and prefectures is contrary to democracy, as the results of the Lower House election in December 2012 demonstrated. In that election, the LDP won 237 out of 300 "small" electoral districts, in each of which a single candidate garnering the plurality of votes wins. It also won 60 seats in 11 regional electoral districts consisting of multiple prefectures in which each party wins seats proportional to the number of votes cast for a party. To win 237 seats (79 percent of 300 "small district" seats), the LDP candidates received a total of only 24.67 percent of votes cast because all votes cast except for the winner in each district become "dead votes." The total number of votes that the LDP received was 1.66 million fewer than in the preceding Lower House election, when it lost badly to the DPJ. In the proportional electoral blocks too, the LDP received 2.2 million fewer votes than in the preceding election. An analysis of the results of the Lower House election in 2014, in which the LDP again won a large majority of seats, shows that the outcome again owed to the electoral system.

The current electoral system was adopted in 1994 and eliminated electoral districts in which between two and four candidates were elected. This change, which increased "dead votes" and favors the LDP, the dominant conservative party, was made because the LDP wanted to find a way to stem the seemingly inexorable declining trend in its electoral strength after the collapse of the economic bubble in 1991. A sufficient number of conservative members of the DPJ and a few small conservative parties who also faced the same trend supported the change.

No less importantly, Japan still has not rectified the long-standing "weight gap" of a vote: a vote in the conservative rural districts "weighs" as much as four times as a vote in the more liberal districts in large cities. In 2011 and 2012 several local courts, and then the Supreme Court, ruled that in several urban electoral districts the existing electoral law "unconstitutionally" deprived voters of their right to the principle of "one person, one vote." However, the courts did not invalidate the election results for the Upper and the Lower Houses in these same years. A very minor change was made in 2013, eliminating five seats in rural districts by enlarging or combining rural districts, but the weight gap remains, with a rural vote still weighing two to almost three times as much as a city vote. In March 2015, five regional high courts in Tokyo, Osaka, Nagoya, Hiroshima and Sendai ruled that the Lower House election in December 2014 had been held "in a state of an unconstitutional vote weight gap," but again, the courts did not invalidate the election results. In April 2016 another change was made to reduce the number of Lower House seats by eliminating six small districts and redrawing the boundaries of four regional districts, both in rural prefectures. However, this change still keeps small districts and the rural vs. urban weight gap of votes remains in excess of two to one, to the undue and constitutionally illegal advantage of the conservative parties.

Germany

What do the Germans need to do to effect a systemic change? The most important change the Germans must make is to end their pursuit of fiscal austerity, which became a constitutional requirement when the Schuldenbremse (debt break) clause was added to the German constitution in 2009. This clause requires both the federal and state governments to balance their budgets, beginning in 2016, and reinforces the small government policy of the Merkel administration, at the costs of preventing the economy from growing at a faster rate and of widening disparity in the distribution of income and wealth.

Today, many German political scientists and pundits seem to believe that, in contrast to many other large democratic countries, Germany's political institutions and practices have no obvious and serious failings. This is mainly because the most contentious case involving the election law was settled in 2013. Germany's Constitutional Court ruled in 2009 that the voting system used in the general election that year had been unconstitutional. In response to the court ruling, the Bundestag changed the complex voting system in 2010, but the Court decided that the changed system was still unconstitutional. Then, in 2013 the Bundestag amended the voting system and it was ruled constitutional.[3]

I am fully aware that those who are more familiar with politics, especially Germany's, than I am, will have many other examples of changes in political institutions and practices that need to be made as an integral part of systemic change in the US, Japan and Germany.

All three countries need to make changes in their political institutions and practices that are integral to effecting a systemic change. This will also be the case for all other developed economies. Changing tax laws and making many other changes in both economic and political institutions and practices will be extremely daunting. The debate will be intense in all of the developed economies. However, it cannot be more difficult than when the first two systemic changes were made. The most crucial decision to be faced is not whether or not to make a systemic change, but how much faster a third systemic change can be made than were the first two.

Can "big government" and democracy coexist?

The argument that a "big government" changes capitalism into socialism is erroneous. It is often ideologically motivated and/ or based on inaccurate use of the term socialism.

First, let us define what are meant by capitalism and socialism. Capitalism is an economic system based on the private ownership of assets, including the means of production, and in which markets determine prices. But to function efficiently, all markets require some regulation.

There are two kinds of socialism. One is Marxist socialism, known as communism, in which most or all of the means of production are owned and controlled by the state. Bureaucracy replaces most markets, and bureaucracy determines the allocation of resources, and thus the quantity of goods and services produced. The extent of private ownership of assets and permitted market activities can differ significantly from one country to another, as seen in the Soviet Union before the 1980s and in China today. Note also that the degree and types of permitted private ownership and market activities also differ over time in all communist economies.

The second kind of socialism is democratic socialism. This is an economic system based on private property ownership and markets, but the state plays a larger role in the economy than it does in capitalism. The role played by the government in a democratic socialist economy can range from nearly as limited as in a capitalist economy to significantly larger. That is, like white gradually becoming black, it is often a matter of subjective judgment whether an economy is called capitalist or democratic socialist.

Many democratic socialists argue that the government needs to own and operate some large industries within a market economy. But in most democratic socialist economies this is a policy aspiration that is not pursued except for railroads and other public utility-related industries because of the inefficiency of state-run businesses. However, in all democratic socialist economies the role played by the government is larger than in a capitalist economy in providing health insurance, providing more generous safety nets to those in need, giving more power to workers, limiting the influence of money on politics and regulating business practices more closely.

But note that over time all capitalist economies have to some extent become democratic socialist. This is evident when observing the transformation of capitalism during the past 150 years. Even the American form of capitalism had become much more democratic socialist by the end of the 1930s. And the American economy has become even more democratic socialist in recent years, as is evident in the criticism by many conservatives of the liberal policies of Democratic administrations.

All of this is to say that what we call a capitalist system has increasingly becoming a matter of semantics or subjective judgment. When Senator Bernard Sanders, a former Democratic candidate for the presidency in 2016, calls himself a democratic socialist, he is only saying that he wishes to adopt economic policies that are more liberal than those that have been adopted by the Democratic Party in the past. The difficulty of defining what is democratic socialism was made evident when Sanders referred to Denmark as his idea of a democratic socialist country and the Danish prime minister responded by saying:

> I know that some people in the US associate the Nordic model with some sort of socialism. But Denmark is far from a socialist economy. Denmark

is a market economy. The Nordic model is an expanded welfare state that is providing a high level of security to the citizens, but it is also a successful market economy.[4]

In this context, the following finding by the Pew Research Center in November 2011 is revealing. When 1,521 Americans were asked for their reaction to the terms capitalism and socialism, 50 percent were positive and 40 percent were negative to the term capitalism, and 30 percent were positive and 60 percent negative to the term socialism. That as many as 40 percent of Americans think negatively about capitalism suggests that they are increasingly thinking that socialism means democratic socialism, whose policies they support. Stated differently, this survey result attests to the fact that the distinction between capitalism and democratic socialism has become blurred because the two systems increasingly overlap.

The foregoing means that it is inaccurate to argue that a larger government changes capitalism into socialism, let alone Marxist socialism. That is, to call an economic system that has private property ownership and markets a socialist system just because it has a larger government is to ignore the reality of how capitalism has changed during the past few centuries.

For most conservatives, the coexistence of capitalism and democracy is not an issue because they believe the two can and do coexist, but some liberals do not think so. Although views among the latter differ, a typical view is that under capitalism, economic policies and practices will inevitably and increasingly reflect the collective interest of those who possess wealth, and thus political power. As a result, the interests of the majority will be increasingly marginalized, and then even ignored, in economic policies and practices. This will necessarily bring about an increased disparity in the distribution of income and wealth, and many other outcomes such as the fraying of safety nets for the needy and a increasing difference in access to education, jobs and many other basic requirements that perpetuates economic disparity, which democracy should be able to prevent. In short, in this view, capitalism and democracy cannot coexist because capitalism will emasculate democracy.

As will be obvious to readers by now, I disagree strongly with the view that capitalism and democracy cannot coexist. This is because, as we have seen, capitalism and democracy have continued to coexist in all developed economies since the 19th century, and especially in the 20th. However, it cannot be denied that we have seen much evidence of capitalism emasculating democracy since the 1980s. This has occurred despite the historical trend of the capitalist democratic system becoming more social democratic. The main reason is because the developed capitalist economies continue to commit the historic folly of pursuing small government" and pro-investment fiscal and monetary policies based on supply-side economics. These policies are futile and anti-egalitarian in the new world of too much stuff. This means that making the third systemic change is necessary in order for the developed economies to return to the historical trend of capitalism becoming more social democratic.

Quality and quantity in GDP growth

Most of those who advocate an alternative economic system to capitalism, as well as many who are focused on a sustainable environment, argue that the most significant flaw of capitalism is its dependence on maintaining economic growth. This view, however, presumes that the method of measuring GDP cannot be significantly changed. Our current method was adopted during the 1930s, when the concept of the gross domestic product was first introduced in the US as a means for devising the economic policies necessary to overcome the effects of the Depression and revive the economy. Simon Kuznets, the American economist who played a major role in establishing the method of calculating GDP in the early 1930s, wrote:

> The valuable capacity of the human mind to simplify a complex situation in a compact characterization becomes dangerous when not controlled in terms of definitely stated criteria. With quantitative measurements especially, the definiteness of the result suggests, often misleadingly, a precision and simplicity

in the outlines of the object measured. Measurements of national income are subject to this type of illusion and resulting abuse, especially since they deal with matters that are the center of conflict of opposing social groups where the effectiveness of an argument is often contingent upon oversimplification.[5]

Distinctions must be kept in mind between quantity and quality of growth, between costs and returns, and between the short and long run. Goals for more growth should specify more growth of what and for what.[6]

This means that even Kuznets considered GDP to be an approximation made under numerous assumptions. Because even an abbreviated explanation of why this is so would be highly technical and far beyond the scope of this book, the following examples serve to show that GDP is just an approximation.

First, the GDP measurement of many kinds of investments is typically based only on a cost basis or on market price, without considering the much harder-to-estimate stream of various types of "benefits" that the economy will gained from these investments into the future. To make this point, good examples are the services provided and goods produced and consumed in the home. This includes everything from unpaid housework and produce from home gardens to care for aging parents. They are not included in GDP even though we are certain that the total market value of such services and goods is in the tens, if not hundreds, of billions of dollars.

Second, in all developed economies the method of calculating GDP is changed periodically in order to increase its accuracy and international comparability. For example, in the US the most recent change was made in 2013 to add the cost of R&D and other costs of "producing" intellectual property (for example, movies, music, many types of arts and books). This change increased GDP by as much as 3 percent.[7]

Theoretically, the market price of any services and goods can be obtained, but obtaining accurate prices and quantities for them is not possible in practice. For example, all types of investments made to prevent further deterioration of the environment are still calculated on a cost basis without adding the virtually impossible-to-calculate stream of future benefits that will accrue to society. This means that we must do our best to debate and devise agreed-upon ways to estimate the future benefits of all societal investments, as is seen most evidently in the case of investment to preserve the sustainability of the environment. Even if we cannot agree how to calculate the future benefits of the investment, we know that they will be incalculably huge.

To ask that an economy not grow or remain in a stasis for any reason, including to protect the environment, is analogous to suggesting that a vibrant tree be changed into a bonsai, an artificially stunted ornamental plant. Economic growth that is achieved both quantitatively and qualitatively must continue. After the third systemic change, capitalism will be able to make technological progress and use resources even more efficiently than today and than in any alternative systems, for the benefit of everyone in the generations to come. What is needed, as an integral part of making the third systemic change of our capitalist democracy, is a serious debate on how to measure GDP.

THIRTEEN

Conclusion

At more than a decade and a half into the 21st century, we see little prospect of the developed economies being able to grow at more than 3 percent per year on a sustained basis or to avoid recurrent bouts of recession. We are already familiar with the very high and rising costs of prolonged stagnation; our economies remain unable to make the investments necessary to meet the needs of society and their democracy itself is threatened.

This despairing reality cannot be changed if we continue to implement the current policies, which are ineffective in the new world of necessary luxuries. We must recognize that we are now living in a new world and change the existing capitalist system as soon as possible. Should we fail to do so, our economies and democracies will not survive and thrive into the future. We know that it is possible to make a systemic change because this was achieved successfully both in Britain and in the US. In both of these systemic changes, the changes made in laws, institutions and practices were ones that at the outset few people thought possible. To think that a third systemic change is impossible is to fail to learn from history.

Still, many readers are likely to argue that making a third systemic change is not possible today because we are not facing either the possibility of revolution, as did Britain during the 19th century, nor all the dire consequences of the Great Depression – such as prolonged mass destitution, a high unemployment rate and many manifestations of a looming political crisis – which confronted the US during the 1930s. However, such thinking is erroneous, because all the developed economies are confronted today with the increasingly real possibility of passing both a political and an environmental tipping point.

To fail to recognize that we are near a political tipping point is to disregard obvious manifestations of the seething rage and desperate frustration of more and more people over the widening disparity in the distribution of income and wealth. When we see these manifestations, which include the declining voter participation rate in elections and the increasing popularity of a proliferation of extremist far Right and far Left political parties, we all know that democracy is increasingly imperiled. And we also know that the governments of these economies have become increasingly ineffectual or even gridlocked. A growing number of young people have become alienated and angst-ridden over their persistent high unemployment rates – which in some countries even exceed 50 percent – and the generally dismal prospects for their future, which have convinced them that the existing political-economic system has failed them.

If the political tipping point is reached, there will be a strong possibility of an election outcome that will bring about radical change in the distribution of income and wealth and the adoption of an economic system that history has shown will be much less efficient than democratic capitalism. If a populist, xenophobic and anti-capitalist political party should win an election, its administration would likely adopt policies that confiscated much of the wealth from the rich, strangled financial institutions and international trade, prohibited immigration and forced through other inchoate populist policies. The result would be an inefficient economy and a decline in the living standard. Once in power, such a government would be very difficult to dislodge. To believe that voters in the developed economies would never elect an ideologically extreme xenophobic populist party is to disregard the lessons of history that include the rises of Nazi Germany and of Hugo Chavez in Venezuela and his counterparts in other countries during the past two centuries.

Not only do we face a looming political debacle, we are also confronted with an impending global environmental calamity. To deny the possibility of passing the environmental tipping point is to willfully ignore all the unmistakable manifestations of the impending calamity. In recent decades we have experienced extreme floods, droughts and unseasonal weather that have been increasing in both frequency and severity. They have already deprived millions of people around the globe of their homes and livelihoods. To say either that the world does not face an environmental calamity or that there is nothing that can be done to avert it is to disbelieve the consensus of scientists and all the evidence of anthropogenic environmental degradation because of short-sighted political and/or economic self-interest. Should we cross the environmental Rubicon, it will make any discussion of political and economic systems superfluous. When the current environmental crisis becomes an environmental cataclysm because no systemic change was made in the developed economies so as to lead a global effort to avert it, what becomes the issue will not be the survival of our system, but the survival of our civilizations.

This book has dealt with the advanced capitalist economies, but we should not ignore developments in the rest of the world, which increase the urgency for our economies to make a systemic change. These developments include the decelerating trend of economic growth that we see today in most emerging economies. The most important example of slowing growth is China, the world's second-largest economy, with which all developed economies have an increasing volume of trade and investment. China now has a very large excess productive capacity in many industries, and at the same time approximately 300 million Chinese have entered into the new world, as is seen from their increased consumption of necessary luxuries. The Chinese economic growth rate is not likely to increase because the country is relying more on pro-investment and easy-money policies. That is, China too is falling into the same trap as the advanced economies. The slow growth of China, which has already become an additional reason for the ongoing persistent stagnation of the developed economies, will certainly be a significant factor in necessitating systemic change for our economies.

The media are full of ideas for simplifying our lifestyles and clearing out our clutter, but these messages are overwhelmed and lost in the enticements to buy the newest version of our electronic devices, to purchase a new car at a low interest rate, to drink water flown in from abroad or to go abroad for a vacation. All of this is at the cost of failing to make the socially necessary investment, investment that is the only way to reinvigorate the developed economies in the new world and that will become possible only by making a systemic change.

Do you really need more T-shirts or the latest smartphone? Or could you pay somewhat higher taxes, depending on your income bracket, so that our physical infrastructure could be upgraded, our education system improved, our healthcare system be made available to all and every effort be made to prevent further degradation of the environment? Do you want to live in a country where you pass the homeless as you walk down the street, face more flood and storm damage every year and see more policies adopted to make the rich richer while everyone else struggles?

I end this book with my sincerest plea to you, the reader. Please do all you can to help make the third systemic change so that you, your children and your grandchildren will not face the world that will result if we fail to do so. Please do all you can to convince others to realize that they too live in this new world in which pro-investment policies and a small government will not only be futile in reinvigorating the economy, but will also be catastrophic for the environment and perilous to democracy. We need as many voters as possible to vote for politicians who will do their best to make the third systemic change of capitalism. The third systemic change is the only way to enable capitalism to endure and thrive and for democracy to become robust in the new world of too much stuff.

Postscript

Much has happened between March 2016 when I completed the manuscript for this book and mid-November 2016 as I write this postscript to take account of the significant developments and new data that have become available over this period, and to introduce some new thoughts – particularly on how culture matters in each country's effort to make a systemic change.

Unfortunately, since many of these developments reaffirm the central argument of this book, the situation in the advanced economies remains basically the same. And thus, in the new world of "too much stuff", a systemic change of capitalism is necessary for capitalism and democracy in the developed economies to survive and thrive into the future.

The most significant developments of the last eight months include the following. On June 23, 2016, the UK voted to leave the European Union. In numerous regional elections held since April in Italy, France and Germany, populist, xenophobic and anti-EU rightwing parties, such as the Five Star Movement in Italy, the National Front in France and the Alternative for Germany, have won significantly more votes than previously. Donald Trump won the election on November 8 in the US, despite his advocacy of demagogic nativist policies and an utterly ludicrous economic policy based on supply-side economics. And the Republicans still control the Senate and the House of Representatives to presage a continuing pursuit of their misguided fiscal and anti-environmental policies as well as appointments of more right-leaning judges at both the Federal and the Supreme Courts with all of the associated consequences. As the recounting of the votes continues, as of November 23, Hillary Clinton, the Democratic presidential nominee had a total of 64,223,958 votes, compared to Republican Trump's 62,206,395. That's a margin of 2,017,563 votes, up about a quarter of a million votes from just the day before. Overall, Clinton has won 48.1 of the popular vote, compared to 46.6 percent for Trump, but she lost the election because of the of the archaic Electoral College system.

There are various reasons for each of these developments. However, the fundamental reason for all of them is that the developed capitalist economies have continued to pursue a counter-productive fiscal policy of tax cuts and austerity, plus a futile super-easy monetary policy. Thus, they suffer from all the consequences of these policies, which include chronic slow economic growth, a wide disparity in the distribution of income and wealth, stagnant real wages, and high "real" rates of unemployment and underemployment. If a systemic change in the advanced economies had been made and these economies no longer faced these consequences, those issues involving stagnant real wages, immigration and the EU membership could not have morphed into barely disguised racism, demagogic proposals for nativist, anti-global trade and other populist demands. People enjoying a steadily increasing real wage, job security and a brighter prospect for their future would not have been likely to vote for Brexit, for the populist, xenophobic parties in Europe or for a demagogic advocate of fallacious supply-side economics for the US presidency.

To demonstrate the continuing urgency of making a systemic change of capitalism in the advanced economies, in the following paragraphs this brief postscript presents the most compelling observations and data to have come to my attention since April 2016. I am also adding a few thoughts that do not appear in the book. I begin with one of the most important recent findings.

In the new world of too much stuff, you will be poorer than your parents

A report entitled "Stagnation Generation: The Case for Renewing the Intergenerational Contract," issued by The Resolution Foundation in London on July 18, 2016, offers a telling analysis of the economic plight of the "millennials" (generally defined as people born between 1982 and 2004). This report was written for the UK but it epitomizes the plight of the millennials in all of the developed economies, where their unemployment and underemployment rates combined are almost double those for the total labor force.

Key points in the report are:

- In the history of industrial capitalism, millennials are at risk of becoming the first generation ever to record lower lifetime earnings than earlier generations. In contrast to the taken-for-granted promise that each generation will be better off than the last, today's 27-year-olds (born in 1988) earn the same amount that 27-year-olds did a quarter of a century ago. That is, in real (inflation-adjusted) terms, a typical millennial has actually earned £8,000 (about $10,400) less during their twenties than those in the preceding generation (often called generation X) earned.
- Lower levels of home ownership among younger generations generate short-term disappointment and longer-term living standard challenges. "Baby boomers" (the demographic cohort born during the post-Second World War baby boom between 1946 and 1964) at age 30 were 50 percent more likely to own their own home than a millennial at the same age.
- In the next four years, the tax and benefit plans in effect in 2016 will take £1.7 billion away from millennials, while giving £1.2 billion to baby boomers, aged between 52 and 70. This means generational fairness has been sacrificed for political reasons.

Simply put, millennials' lifetime earnings are lower than those of the preceding generation because of the persistent slow economic growth caused by the arrival of the new world of too much stuff.

There are numerous undeniable corollaries of the report's findings that do not appear in the report but are nevertheless obvious. Millennials' reduced lifetime earnings limit their education and delay their marriages, thus reducing the birth rate (that is, total fertility rate, or TFR), which has various serious consequences that were discussed in Chapter Two of this book. And because of the prospect of earning less than their parents, they are becoming disenchanted with politics and the existing capitalist system, as evidenced in their much lower rates of voting compared to older generations.

Because of these developments, in order to make a systemic change in the US, Americans must grapple with the deeply embedded sociocultural myth of "the American dream", the dream that anyone can succeed financially and that each succeeding generation will be better off financially than the preceding one. The first half of the myth is indeed just a myth, and the idea that each succeeding generation will be better off has now also become a myth in the new world of too much stuff.

However, these myths endure in the US for two major reasons. First, they are intentionally perpetuated by the economically and politically powerful, who endeavor to preserve the existing capitalist system. Second, a majority of Americans, including half of those aged between 18 and 29, still seem to believe in them despite the empirical evidence to the contrary.[1] Thus, those Americans who see the necessity of making a systemic change in their capitalism must begin by convincing their fellow citizens that the American dream is a myth perpetrated by those who wish to preserve the existing American capitalist system. This task will be even more daunting than persuading voters that tax-reducing supply-side economics is totally fallacious, because the American dream is far more deeply rooted in the American psyche than supply-side economics.

Income and wealth distributions are still unequal and becoming more so.

On September 13, 2016, the US Census Bureau reported that during 2015 Americans reaped the largest economic gains in recent decades as poverty fell, health insurance coverage spread and incomes rose sharply for households on every rung of the economic ladder, ending years of income stagnation. The median household's income in 2015 was $56,500, up 5.2 percent from the previous year — the largest single-year increase since recordkeeping began in 1967. The share of Americans living in poverty also posted the sharpest decline in decades.

However, on close reading, it quickly becomes evident that the upbeat tone of the report is misleading because the comparisons used and the focus on averages obscures the reality. While the economy finally seems to be moving in the right direction, the real incomes of most American households were still 2.4 percent lower than at the absolute peak reached in 1999, and median household income was still 1.6 percent lower than in 2007, adjusting for inflation. And in 2015, the poorest 10 percent of households were still poorer than they were in 1989. Across the entire bottom 60 percent of the distribution, households are taking home a smaller slice of the pie than they did in the 1960s and 1970s. The 3.4 percent of income that households in the bottom fifth took home last year was less than the 5.8 percent they had in 1974. With their share shrinking with almost every economic cycle, it is hardly a surprise that it takes longer for them to experience any income gains at all. In contrast, households in the top 5 percent have profited nicely from America's economic performance. In 2015, they took in $350,870, on average. That is 4.9 percent more than in 1999 and 37.5 percent more than in 1989.

On June 23, 2016, the *Guardian*, a British daily, reported that the number of "high net worth individuals" – those with investable assets of at least $1 million – exceeded 15 million in 2015. The US had the most such individuals at 4.5 million. Japan was second with 2.7 million, and Germany third with 1.2 million. Their numbers grew in 2015 by 2 percent in the US; by 11 percent in Japan; and by 5 percent in Germany.

In Germany, a federation representing 10,000 social welfare groups warned on March 18, 2016,[2] that nearly one in six German residents remained at risk of being trapped in relative poverty. (The term "relative poverty" used across the EU refers to anyone, child or adult, who lives on less than 60 percent of the medium income as measured statistically). In Germany, that threshold is 917 euros ($1,015) per month for a single person and 1,192 euros ($1,310) for a single parent with a child under six. The results overall continue to point to massive inequality in German society, despite glowing data such as the recent announcement that in 2015 Germany recorded its highest federal budget surplus since reunification, despite its taking in more than 1 million refugees.

Worse still, an article entitled "Anxieties about social justice may come to dominate the election next year" appeared in *The Economist* of October 29–November 4, 2016. This article observed, "When it comes to the distribution of wealth, Germany is near the top of the inequality scale, behind only Austria in the eurozone. The top 10% of German households own about 60% of the country's wealth, whereas the bottom 20% own nothing, or are in debt. This is largely explained by Germans renting homes more than owning, and by relying more on government pensions."

Why is income inequality increasing in the developed economies despite economic growth, however anemic?

The real unemployment rate is not falling and wages are not rising

According to the data from the US Bureau of Labor Statistics (the BLS), the US unemployment rate was 4.9 percent in September 2016, exactly the same as in September 1997. However, this does not mean the labor market in 2016 is as healthy as it was in the late 1990s when the economy was growing at around 4 percent. As was discussed in Chapter Seven, the unemployment rate announced by the BLS is not the same as the broader measure called the U-6 unemployment rate, which accounts for the labor participation rate. That is, in September 2016, only 62.8 percent of Americans aged 16 or older were in the labor force compared to 67.2 percent in September 1997, despite the fact that in 2016 many involuntary part-timers were counted as working. The reason for this fall is that so many discouraged workers had quit looking for jobs. Thus the U-6 unemployment rate in July 2016 was actually 9.7 percent, nearly double that reported by the Bureau of Labor Statistics. The most recent available BLS unemployment rate I could obtain was for September 2016 when it had risen to 5.1 percent, while the U-6 rate remained at 9.7 percent.

Japan also has a seemingly very low rate of unemployment at the same time that the   real wage is not rising, and is even declining for many workers. When the rate of unemployment is low, it is expected that wages will rise as employers compete for good workers. But this anomalous situation of stagnant real wages when the unemployment rate is very low can be easily explained. Most workers in Japan when faced with unemployment will take non-regular, lower-paying, often part-time jobs, whereas workers in other countries in the same situation will receive unemployment insurance or welfare. But in Japan, the non-regular jobs pay better than unemployment insurance, which is neither generous in the amount paid or in its eligibility conditions by international standards.[3]

For example, in 2014, total employment in Japan rose by 1.03 million persons while the number of regular employees declined by 380,000. This occurred because the number of non-regular part-time employees rose by 530,000, of *arubaito* (from *arbeiters* in German, meaning temporary workers) by 350,000, and of contract workers (those employed on a semi-permanent basis by renewing successive short-term contracts) by 530,000. In all of these categories, wages are lower and employment conditions poorer than those of regular employees, as described in Chapter Eight.[4] In the same year, as many as 70 percent of unemployed Japanese took lower-paying and/or part-time jobs rather than receive unemployment insurance.[5]

Why so many Japanese are willing to accept low wages, short hours, poor working conditions, and few or no benefits can be understood by the social opprobrium – "shame" – of accepting unemployment insurance, which most Japanese regard as social charity or living on the dole. While shame exists in every culture, it is a particularly strong motivator in Japan with its long history of closed communities in which no one wanted to become a burden on one's neighbors. Thus, Japanese will accept government aid only as a last resort.[6]

The proponents of pro-investment fiscal and monetary policies tout the declining unemployment as their major accomplishment by ignoring the real rate of unemployment and underemployment, and stagnant real wages, all of which maintain or even increase the disparity in income distribution.

In short, the proponents of these ineffective policies keep cherry-picking the data, while ignoring all the increasingly negative ramifications of their pro-investment policies.

The undesirable effects of printing money are proliferating

Central banks continue their super-easy monetary policy – that is, printing money – although it is increasingly threatening the insurance industry. This industry is a crucial cog in the financial system, but the easy monetary policy reduces returns on investments, as noted in Chapter Four. This is now most clearly seen in the mounting difficulties that both public and private pension funds today face in all of the advanced economies. Among the legions of readily available observations and data that attest to this fact, the following quotations are most revealing:

> The UK has run up a national pension deficit of more than £400 billion ($518 billion) over the past decade, becoming the biggest liability to the economy.
>
> Even worse, the Bank of England's decision last week to cut the interest rate to record lows and begin a bond buying programme of quantitative easing means the deficit is only going to get bigger. HSBC's head of European credit strategy Jamie Stuttard warned in a recent note that Governor Mark Carney's monetary policy move means: "The pension issue is essentially kicked down the road for somebody else to sort out."[7]

> On September 21, 2016 the policymaking committee of the Bank of Japan decided to modify the framework of its policies to pay much closer attention to the long-term interest rate while retaining its negative interest rate policy and its policy to buy government bonds. This was done because the long-term interest rate has sharply declined due to the negative interest

policy and is reducing the earnings of pension funds. The new policy goal is to let the long-term rate rise while keeping all other rates as close as possible to zero percent.[8]

There are many studies in the US as well that reveal the same problem. Although the data are for 2015, one of the most succinct is the following:

> For many former state workers, a monthly public pension check is their bread and butter in retirement. But the gap between what states have promised retirees and how much is saved to fund those payments has grown according to a new report from Pew Charitable Trusts. States are short $968 billion for their pension systems, an increase of $54 billion over the year before. When debts from local programs are taken into account, the total shortfall tops $1 trillion, according to the report. Three states – Illinois, Kentucky and Connecticut – have less than half of their pension programs funded. Illinois is in the hole by more than $100 billion.[9]

The ultra-low or negative interest rate policy is increasingly distorting the normal function of the financial system, as noted in Chapter Four, but it is also perverting the system by reducing the private ownership of firms, which is the prevalent ownership in a sound capitalist system. This is occurring in all of the developed economies where the central bank is pursuing quantitative easing by buying stocks. However, it is seen most clearly in Japan where the ownership of stocks by the Bank of Japan has been steadily increasing since 2013 as the Bank has aggressively pursued a pro-investment monetary policy.

> The Bank of Japan's controversial march to the top of shareholder rankings in the world's third-largest equity market is picking up pace. Already a top-five owner of 81 companies listed in Japan's Nikkei 225

Stock Average, the BOJ is on course to become
the No. 1 shareholder in 55 of those firms by the
end of next year.... While bulls have cheered the
tailwind from BOJ purchases, opponents say the
central bank is artificially inflating equity valuations
and undercutting efforts to make public companies
more efficient.[10]

On October 12, 2016, the *Asahi Shimbun*, Japan's major
newspaper, reported the following fact that should make all of
us concerned with the future of capitalism and democracy in
the advanced economies take note. On October 7, the amount
of Japanese government bonds bought by the Bank of Japan
exceeded 4 trillion dollars (calculated at 100 yen to the dollar.)
This is about 40 percent of the total outstanding national debt
of Japan, which exceeds 250 percent of GDP. And the Bank of
Japan is still buying almost all of the new government bonds
sold as it continues its policy of increasing the money supply
much more aggressively than either the ECB and or the Fed
has been doing.

What the Bank of Japan is doing is monetizing the debt
by buying government bonds, which usually leads inevitably
to hyperinflation, as occurred in Germany during the early
1920s when the government printed money to finance its debt.
However, as seen in the inflation rate in Japan today, which
remains much lower than 2 percent, what the Bank is doing is
not likely to cause hyperinflation. However, it is enabling the
Abe government to pursue its pro-investment policy, which
is creating a bubble in the price of stocks and other assets and
thereby increasing the disparity in the distribution of income
and wealth. That is, the monetization of debt is enabling Japan
to delay making the systemic change to its capitalism necessary
to enable the government to increase tax revenues to invest to
meet societal needs, the only way to reinvigorate the economy
in the new world of too much stuff.

Japan is a canary in a coalmine. All of the other developed
economies where the debt-to-GDP ratio is steadily rising
as their central banks too monetize their debt must learn

from what is happening to Japan as it pursues its delusional Abenomics.

Germany cannot continue fiscal austerity and its huge trade surplus

Just as Japan needs to abandon Abenomics, Germany too needs to change its pro-export, low wage policy and high saving rate. This was made even more evident on September 6, 2016, when Reuters reported that Germany's current account surplus is likely to hit a new record of $310 billion (278 billion euros) in 2016, overtaking that of China to again become the world's largest. And on the same day, the Munich-based Ifo Center for Economic Studies said, "The German current account surplus is based on trade in goods, and exports exceeded imports by $159 billion in the first half of the year, mainly due to strong demand from other European countries. The German surplus would be equivalent to around 8.9 percent of gross domestic product." A percentage this high would once again breach the European Commission's recommended upper threshold of 6 percent.

Without a systemic change, Germany will continue to pursue fiscal austerity and demand others in the European Union to do the same. This is because for most Germans, frugality, or abhorrence of debt, is culturally deep-rooted. This is seen in their support of Merkel's fiscal austerity policy and in Germany's high saving rate. Data from the German central bank show that the household saving rate in Germany was 9.70 percent in the second quarter of 2016. The rate averaged 11.88 percent from 1960 until 2016, reaching an all-time high of 17.30 percent in the second quarter of 1975. This persistently high saving rate, which reduces domestic demand, explains why Germany consistently maintains the highest per capita trade surplus in the world, as was detailed in Chapter Nine.

One cannot deny that the high saving rate and the huge trade surplus of Germany are due in part to its cultural tradition, as exemplified by the fact that in German, *Schuld* means both "debt" and "guilt." ("I feel guilty" in German is "Ich fühle mich schuldig.") And "austerity," a commonly used word in all other developed economies, does not exist in German. They had to create a new word, *"austerität,"* which few people use, least of all Chancellor Angela Merkel. She prefers to speak of *"sparpolitik"* which translates as "the politics of saving money", or of spending it "sparingly" – and *"sparsamkeit"* (frugality). Both terms have positive meanings, and policies based on them are seen as good policies. Conversely, policies not based on "sparpolitik" are necessarily regarded as bad policies. This was the main reason why the Schuldenbremse (debt break) clause was added to the German constitution in 2009, mandating both the federal and state governments to balance their budgets beginning in 2016, as was discussed in Chapter Twelve.

The above means that to end fiscal austerity in order to help the economy grow and to prevent widening the disparity in the distribution of income and wealth, and even more importantly, to make a systemic change in German capitalism, Germans must come to terms with their cultural tradition of frugality. They must come to understand that it will stand in the way of adopting an effective fiscal policy and that having a larger government that taxes and invests more to meet the societal needs is the only way to make German capitalism endure and prosper into the future.

The more things change, the more they remain the same

On October 30, 2016, Spain's Socialist Party, its second largest party, agreed to abstain instead of voting against the formation of a minority government led Mariano Rajoy of the conservative People's Party. This meant that after 10 months, Spain finally has a government and no longer has to hold the election scheduled for December 2016. However, as the minority government was formed by the People's Party together with smaller parties which hold very diverse views from the People's Party on many issues, there is no doubt that Spain will continue to have an unstable government trying its best to pursue fiscal austerity and cope with an unemployment rate that still hovers around 20 percent.[11]

Sadly, Spain is no exception. Without a systemic change, however frequently the government is changed in all developed economies, they will continue to have a government that is ineffective in reinvigorating the economy, thus prone to political gridlock or paralysis, attesting to the validity of the French saying "Plus ça change, plus c'est la même chose."

Projected growth rates of the developed economies remain dismal

After examining the economic growth rate of the advanced economies in 2016 to date and that projected for 2017 by the IMF, the OECD, the World Bank and others, we must conclude that slow growth rate for all of the developed economies continues as 2016 nears its end. The annualized growth rate of the third quarter (July to September) was unusually high at 2.9 percent for the US, 0.6 percent for Japan, 1.7 percent for Germany, and for the Euro area as a whole, 1.5 percent, with Italy growing only at 0.8 percent. The average projected growth rate for 2017 is only 2 percent for the US, 0.8 percent for Japan, 1.2 percent for Germany, and for the Euro area just 1.2 percent because it includes Italy, which is projected to grow at only 0. 7 percent. No respected organization, such as those noted above, is predicting a faster growth rate in the foreseeable future. The readers of this book know all of this is to be expected in the new world of too much stuff and these figures reinforce the urgency of making a systemic change of capitalism as soon as possible.

I end this brief postscript with the following: It is surreal that at the end of 2016 we are still debating pro-investment fiscal and monetary policies in the developed economies, with no politicians or pundits explicitly recognizing that we now live in the "new world of too much stuff." It is my hope that this book will be useful in helping as many voters as possible in the developed economies realize that a systemic change is necessary for our capitalism and democracy to survive and thrive. We need to increase tax revenues in order to make the investments necessary to meet societal needs instead of reducing taxes and printing more money to produce more "necessary luxuries," and thereby increasing the disparities in the distribution of income and wealth and further degrading the environment.

Notes

Chapter One

[1] Lanny Ebenstein, *Chicagonomics: The Evolution of Chicago Free Market Economics* (St. Martin's Press, 2015), is recommended to readers interested in an in-depth, readable discussion of the role of government in an economy. Chicagonomics refers to the political and economic analysis supporting "a small government" policies that was led by Milton Friedman, Professor of Economics at the University of Chicago and a Nobel laureate.

[2] Arthur C. Brooks, *The Conservative Heart: How to Build a Fairer, Happier and More Prosperous America* (Broadside Books, 2015), pp. 187–8. The author is president of the American Enterprise Institute, a major conservative think tank. As the source of the specific information contained in the above quote, he cites Haley Geffen, "The Napkin Doodle That Launched the Supply-side Revolution," *Bloomberg Business*, December 4, 2014.

Chapter Two

[1] Amy Novotney, *American Psychological Association Journal*, July–August, 2008, Vol. 39, No. 7, p. 40.

[2] Supermarket Statistics, Brain Hosting, June 2013.

[3] Nihon Dentsu Inc., "Advertising Expenditures in Japan," www.dentsu.com/knowledgeanddata/index.html

[4] Marie Kondo, *Jinsei ga tokimeku katazuke no mahout*, Sunmark Shuppan, 2011, translated into English as *The Life-Changing Magic of Tidying Up*, (Ten Speed Press, 2014).

Chapter Three

[1] OECD, *The Annual Report*, September 19, 2015, p. 61.

[2] Citizens for Tax Justice reports, 2013 and 2015.

[3] *Der Spiegel*, May 21, 2013.

[4] Sozialpolitic Aktuell.de, October 2015.

[5] The National Federation of Independent Business, *The Annual Credit Availability Survey*, 2012, p. 14.

Chapter Four

[1] Op-ed article in the *Washington Post*, November 5, 2010.

[2] *Nihon Keizai Shinbun* (Japan's *Wall Street Journal*), February 11, 2013.

[3] "Who Benefits from QE?" *Financial Times*, August 23, 2012.

[4] The efficient market hypothesis has a few critical caveats, such as that those who have better information or better analyses than others could "beat" the market in a short run. An excellent, albeit highly technical, discussion of the hypothesis is found in Eugene F. Fama, "Efficient Capital Markets: A Review of Theory and Empirical Work," *The Journal of Finance*, Vol. 25, 1970.

[5] Interested readers are referred to a readable article, entitled "The Nobel Prize Is a Three-way Split," on the works and views of the three in the October 19, 2013 issue of *The Economist*.

[6] "As Conference Ends, Economists Give Clashing Views," Yahoo News, August 24, 2014.

[7] For example, see the article entitled "Fed's Lone Dissenter: No 'Hawkish' Turn," *Wall Street Journal*, March 21, 2014.

[8] *Asahi Shinbun*, November 24, 2014, and *Nihon Keizai Shinbun*, February 4, 2016.

[9] Yasusuke Murakami, *Sangyou shakai no byori* (The Pathology of Industrial Economies), republished in 2010 in the classic book series of Chuo-Koron Publishing Co., p. 347.

[10] When an economy is suffering from high unemployment, it is possible to argue that devaluation benefits the economy. But this argument is valid only in the short term, and assuming that trading partners will not retaliate with competitive devaluation of their own currencies.

[11] In repatriating loans and investments, the American investors sold local currencies and bought dollars, and less investment and fewer loans means less demand for local currencies.

[12] Paul Krugman and Koichi Hamada, *2020nen Seikai Keizai no Shousha to Haisha* [*Victors and Losers in the World Economy in 2020*] (Kodansha Publishing, 2016), p. 222.

Chapter Five

[1] Paper presented by Emmanuel Saez and Thomas Piketty at the 13th Jacques Polak Annual Research Conference hosted by the International Monetary Fund, Washington, D.C., November 8–9, 2012.

[2] Milton and Rose Friedman, *Free to Choose*, Harcourt Press, 1980, p. 148.

[3] Robert E. Lucas Jr., *The Industrial Revolution; Past and Future* (Federal Reserve Bank of Minneapolis, 2004), p. 204.

[4] Joseph Stiglitz, *The New York Times,* January 20, 2013.

[5] Paul Krugman, *The New York Times*, December 15, 2013.

[6] Thomas Piketty, *Capital in the 21st Century* (Harvard University Press, 2013), pp. 21–3 and pp. 245–8.

[7] The U.S. Census Bureau, "Income and Poverty in the United States," September 2014.

[8] The Pew Research Center, "Income Trends and Gaps," 2013.

[9] *Forbes*, June 18, 2013.

[10] *New York Times*, September 22, 2015.

[11] Emmanuel Saez and Gabriel Zucman, *Wealth Inequality In the United States since 1913*, National Bureau of Economic Research, October 2013, p. 37.

[12] Poverty in Japan, *The Global Intelligence*, April 3, 2012; see https://theglobalintelligence.com/2012/04/03/poverty-in-japan/

[13] Federal Statistical Office, Wiesbaden, 2012.

[14] OECD, *Growing Unequal? Income Distribution and Poverty in OECD Countries* (Paris, 2008).

[15] The figures are for the number of millionaires and billionaires (defined as people who have at least a million or a billion dollars to invest) in France and Spain estimated from the data compiled by Credit Swiss, the Royal Bank of Scotland and the American magazine *Forbes*.

[16] Martin Gilens and Benjamin I. Page, "Testing Theories of American Politics: Elites, Interest Groups and Average Citizens," *Perspective on Politics*, Vol. 12, No. 3, September 2014.

Chapter Six

[1] *The Week*, August 11, 2014.

[2] The American Society of Civil Engineers, *The Annual Assessment Report,* 2014.

[3] *Nikkei Business*, November 23, 2012.

[4] *Der Spiegel*, September 18, 2013.

[5] DIW, The German Institute of Economic Research, *A Report on Infrastructural Investments*, June 2013.

[6] "Flood Risk from Climate Change," *New York Times*, September 21, 2014.

[7] "Higher Water Mark", *The Economist*, January 17, 2015.

[8] Antonio Guterres, in a speech at the Global Futures Initiative held at Georgetown University, Washington, D.C. on November 23, 2015.

[9] R. Russell, *London Fogs* (London, 1880), p. 6, as quoted from *The Dictionary of Victorian London*, which can be accessed on the internet.

[10] Data Blog, *The Guardian*, July 16, 2013; http://www.theguardian.com/news/datablog/interactive/2013/jul/16/carbon-emissions-carbon-tax

[10] *Fifth Annual Assessment* of the IPCC (the Intergovernmental panel on Climate Change of the UN), 2014, Chapters 1, 2, 13 and 31.

Chapter Seven

[1] For an extended discussion of the argument and sources of data, see Kozo Yamamura, *The Economic Emergence of Modern Japan* (Cambridge University Press, 1977); Yasusuke Murakami, *An Anti-Classical Political Economic Analysis: A Vision for the New Century* (Stanford University Press, 1996); and Gunter Heiduk and Kozo Yamamura, eds, *Technological Competition and Interdependence* (University of Washington Press, 1990).

[2] Katharine Bradbury, *Trends in U.S. Family Income Mobility, 1969–2006*, Federal Reserve Bank of Boston, Working Paper No. 11-10, Boston, MA, October 20, 2011. See also, "Social Immobility: Climbing The Economic Ladder Is Harder in the U.S. than in Most European Countries," *The Huffington Post Politics*, September 21, 2011.

[3] The US Department of Justice, Bureau of Justice Statistics, "Prisoners in 2013," June 30, 2014.

[4] Bloomberg News, December 30, 2015.

[5] Steven Rattner, "For Tens of Millions, Obamacare Is Working," *New York Times*, February 22, 2015.

[6] David Brooks, "Health Care Trends Show Costs Rising More Slowly," *New York Times*, November 9, 2015.

[7] A report from Accenture cited by CNN Money, April 14, 2013.

[8] To better understand the issues involved in measuring "real" unemployment, a very useful article to read is "Economists Do Not Agree about How to Measure Unemployment," by Danny Vinik, *New Republic.com*, March 17, 2014.

[9] Jim Clifton, "The Big Lie: 5.6% Unemployment," Gallup News, February 3, 2015.

[10] The Congressman, Kevin Yoder, did not deny this. CNN News, December 16, 2014.

[11] Gallup News Organization's "Employment data tracking."

Chapter Eight

[1] For further observations and analyses of the 1980s, see: Yukio Noguchi and Kozo Yamamura, eds., *US–Japan Macroeconomic Relations in the 1980s* (University of Washington Press, 1996).

[2] Bank of Japan, Kinyu seisaku no gaiyo (The outline of monetary policy, www.boj.)

[3] *Yomiuri Shinbun*, December 22, 2014.

[4] This is a translation of Abe's words as quoted in *Sekai,* a major Japanese monthly, August 2014, p. 106.

[5] *Nihon Keizai Shinbun*, December 15, 2014.

[6] *Japan Times*, April 13, 2015.

Chapter Nine

[1] The CDU has a sister conservative party in Bavaria, the Christian Social Union (CSU), which is a de facto regional branch of the CDU. Thus,

they are often referred to as the CDU/CSU. In this chapter CDU refers to the CDU/CSU.

[2] *The Economist*, June 15, 2013.

[3] DIW, *Income and Wealth Inequality after the Financial Crisis: The Case of Germany* (Berlin, 2015), p. 371.

[4] Although the rate can be set at a higher level as more and more states are doing since 2014, the nationally enforced rate still remains at $7.25.

[5] Reuters, April 8, 2016.

[6] For interested readers, the following two books will be useful to better understand recent developments in both in Germany and Japan: Kozo Yamamura and Wolfgang Streeck, eds., *Germany and Japan: The Future of Nationally Embedded Capitalism in a Global Economy* (Cornell University Press, 2001) and Wolfgang Streeck and Kozo Yamamura, eds., *The End of Diversity? Prospects for German and Japanese Capitalism* (Cornell University Press, 2003).

Chapter Ten

[1] Reuters, France News, August 26, 2014.

[2] *Le Monde*, September 21, 2014.

[3] The High Pay Centre, an independent research institute in the UK, August 19, 2014.

[4] Quoted in an article by Roger Cohen, "Trying to Reinvent Italy," *New York Times*, December 14, 2014.

[5] *The Economist*, August 10, 2013.

[6] Positive Universe, Monthly Archives, January 2015, http:// positiveuniverse.com/2015/01/.

Chapter Eleven

[1] The major sources consulted in summarizing this first example were: Jeremy Black and Donald MacRaild, *Nineteenth-Century Britain* (Palgrave Macmillan, 2003); Norman McCord, *British History, 1815–1906* (Oxford University Press, 1991); Roy Jenkins, *Gladstone* (Macmillan, 1995); Eugenio F. Biagini, *Gladstone* (Macmillan, 2000); H.C.G. Matthew, *Gladstone, 1809–1874* (Clarendon, 1986); Richard Shannon, *Gladstone, 1809–1865* (Hamish Hamilton, 1982); and F.W. Hirst, *Gladstone as Financier and Economist* (Ernest Benn, 1931).

[2] Among numerous works consulted for this second example, the most useful were: Richard Hofstadter, *The Progressive Movement, 1900–1915* (Prentice-Hall, 1963); Lewis L. Gould, *America in the Progressive Era, 1890–1914* (Pearson Education Ltd, 2001); Alexander Hicks, *Social Democracy and Welfare Capitalism: A Century of Income Security Politics* (Cornell University Press, 2000); Robert F. Himmelberg, *The Great Depression and the New Deal,* (Greenwood, 2000); Jonathan Hughes and Louis Cain, *American Economic History* (Pearson Books, 2011); and Benjamin Roth, *The Great Depression: A Diary* (Pearson Books, 2010).

Chapter Twelve

[1] The author was chairman of the Council of Economic Advisors under Richard Nixon and Gerald Ford.

[2] Thomas Piketty, *Capital in the 21st Century* (Harvard University Press, 2014), p. 528.

[3] Since it is not possible to explain the extremely complex changes that were made by the amendment, here only the following is added. The 2013 amendments added what are known as "over-hung" equalization seats (*Ausgleichsmandate*) to achieve a fully proportional allocation of Bundestag seats among qualifying parties that have won at least 5 percent of the votes cast for the party, so as to neutralize any disparities resulting from the allocation of *Ausgleichsmandate*. The Germans cast two votes, one for a candidate and one for a party.

[4] Google News, Policy & Politics, October 31, 2015, report on Prime Minister Lars Rasmussen's remarks made at Harvard's Kennedy School of Government on hearing Sanders' comments on Denmark on the previous day.

[5] Simon Kuznets, "National Income of 1929 to 1932," 73rd US Congress, 1934, 2nd session, Senate document no. 124, p. 7.

[6] Simon Kuznets, "How To Judge Quality," *The New Republic*, October 20, 1962, p. 28.

[7] Bureau of Economic Analysis, U.S. Department of Commerce, "Changes to How the U.S. Economy is Measured Roll Out," July 2013.

Postscript

[1] When Harvard's Institute of Politics asked 18- to 29-year-olds if they considered the American dream to be alive or dead, the result was evenly split. About half said they considered the American dream alive and well for them personally. About half said it was dead as a doornail: *The Washington Post*, December 10, 2015.

[2] See www.theocal.de

[3] For details, see The Ministry of Health, Labor and Welfare, *Kaigai Jousei Houkokusho [A Report on Overseas Conditions]*, 2016, pp. 134–42, which presents details of conditions for unemployment insurance that are significantly more stringent than in most economies in the OECD.

[4] The data are from The Statistics Bureau of the Ministry of Internal Affairs and Communications, *Shugou Kouzou Kihon Chosa [A Survey on Employment Structure]*, December, 2014.

[5] In 2014, the ratio was 59 percent in the US, where the conditions for getting unemployment insurance are far more stringent than in Europe (for example, the ratio was 20 percent in France and 6 percent in Germany): International Institute for Labor Studies, *The Financial and Economic Crisis: A Decent Work Response*, 2015, p.16.

[6] For those who read Japanese, Makoto Yuasa's *Hontou ni Komatta Hito no Tameno Seikatsu Hogo [Welfare Payments for Those in Real*

Need] (Doubunkan Publishing, 2007), contains discussions useful in understanding why Japanese are ashamed to accept welfare payments for socio-cultural reasons.

7 Business Insider.com, August 13, 2016.

8 *Asahi Shimbun*, September 22, 2016.

9 CNN, *Money*, http://money.cnn.com/2015/07/14/retirement/worst-state-pensions.

10 NEWSMAX/Finance, "Japan's Central Bank Rising To Become Country's Biggest Shareholder," August 27, 2016.

11 www.thelocal.es. For a detailed discussion of the reasons for the expected instability and ineffectiveness of the new Rajoy government, see: "How much can Mariano Rajoy do?" *The Economist*, October 29–November 4, 2016.

Index

Page references for notes are followed by n